Enchanted Faces Coloring Book

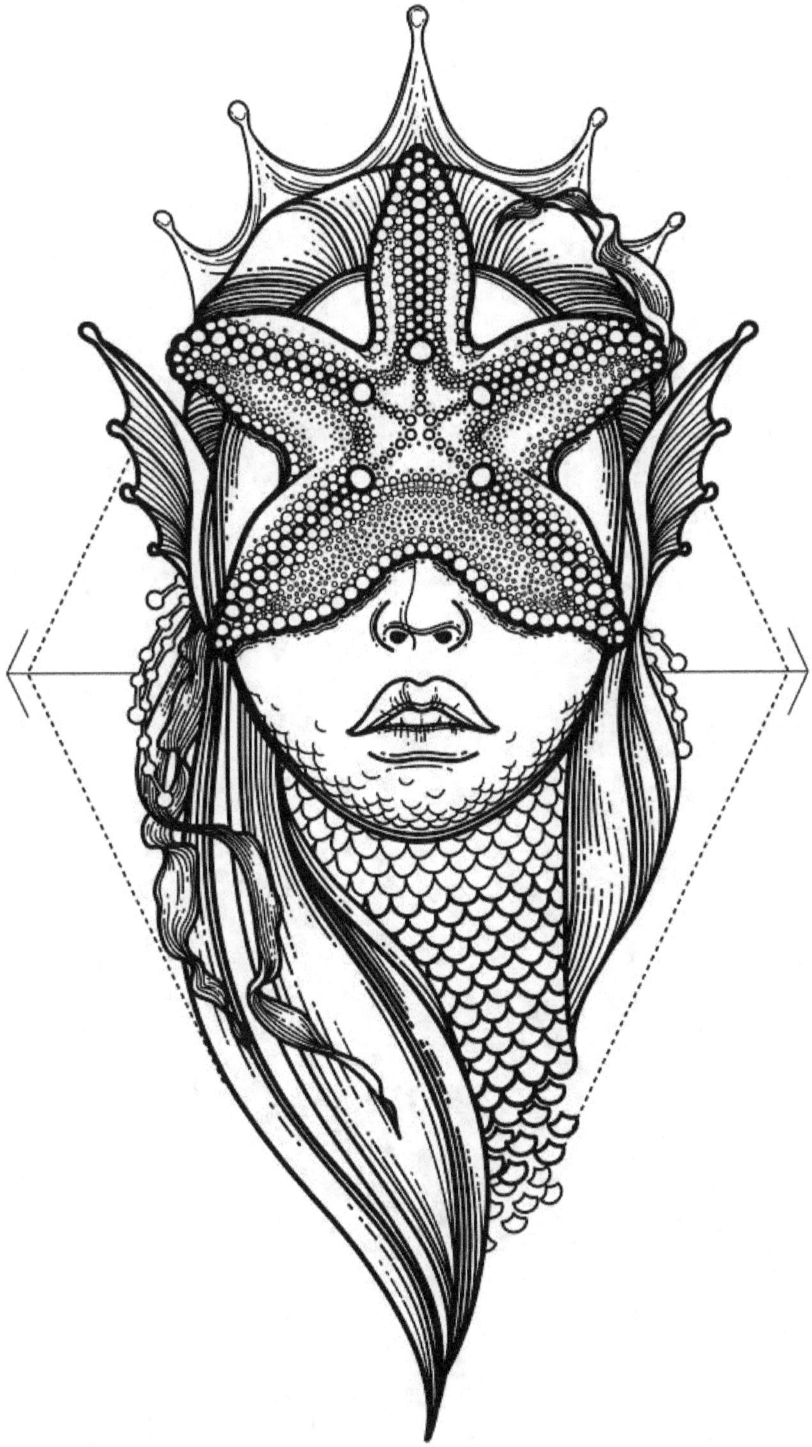

Copyright © 2020 Katrin Stark
ALL RIGHTS RESERVED

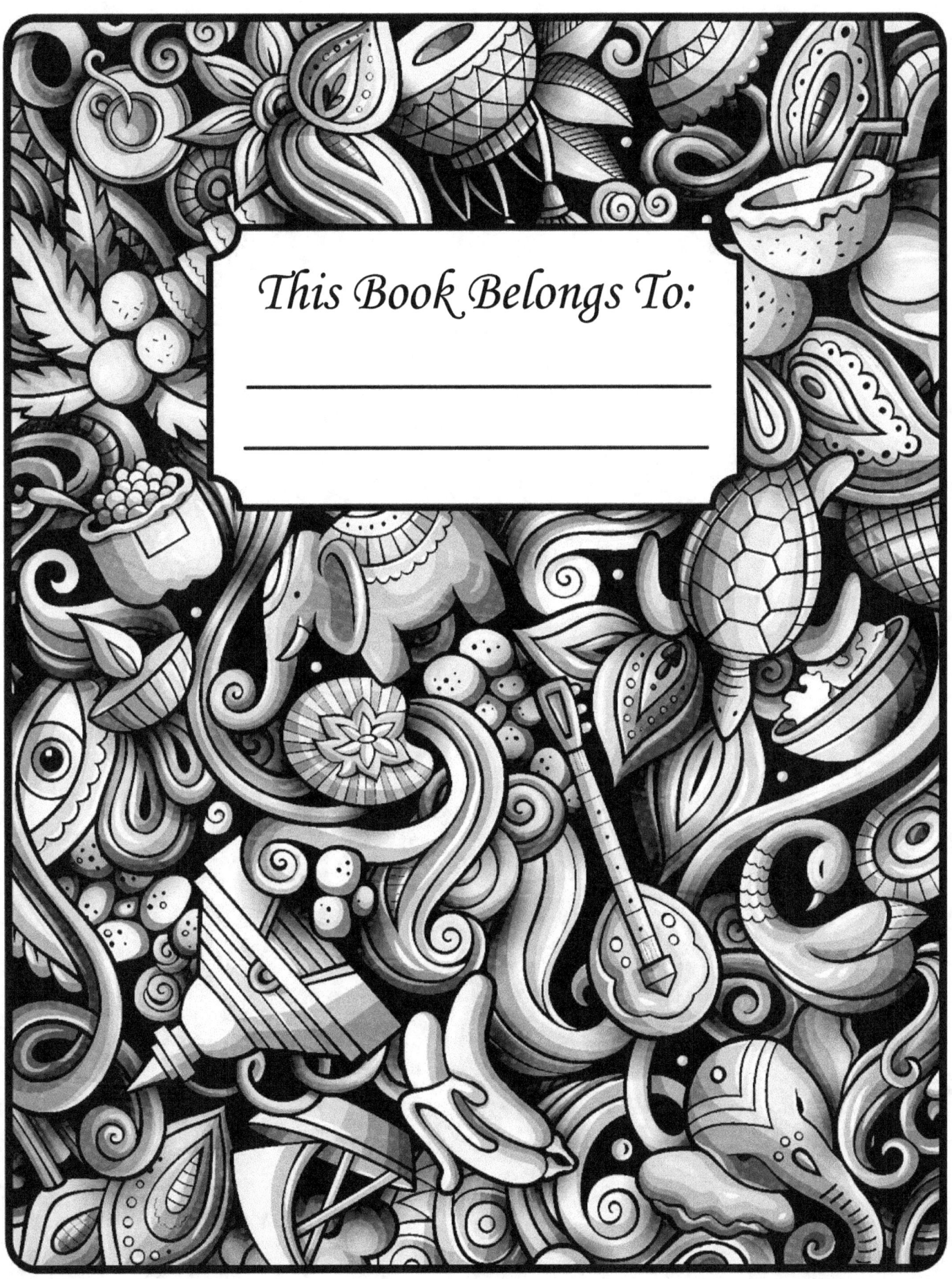

Color Test Page

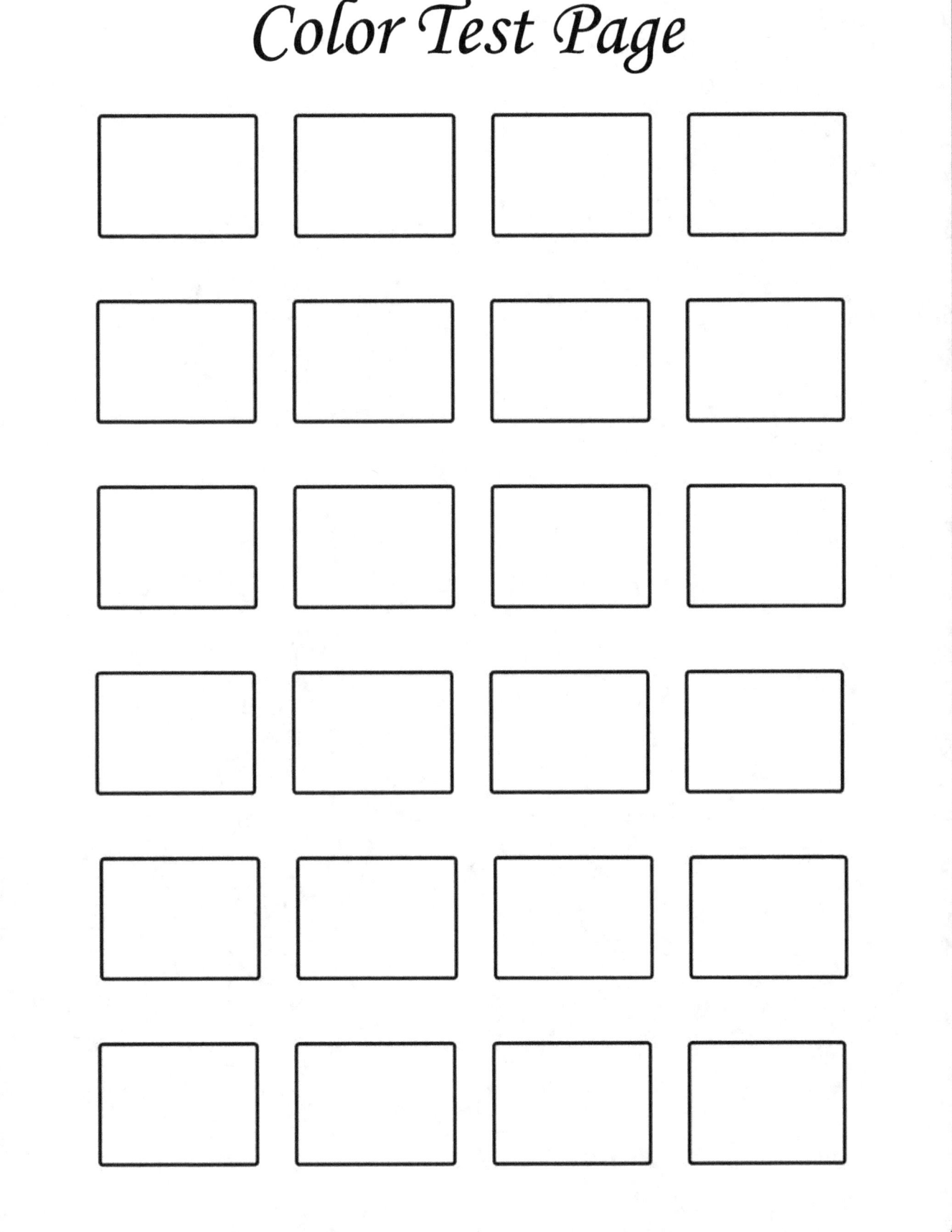

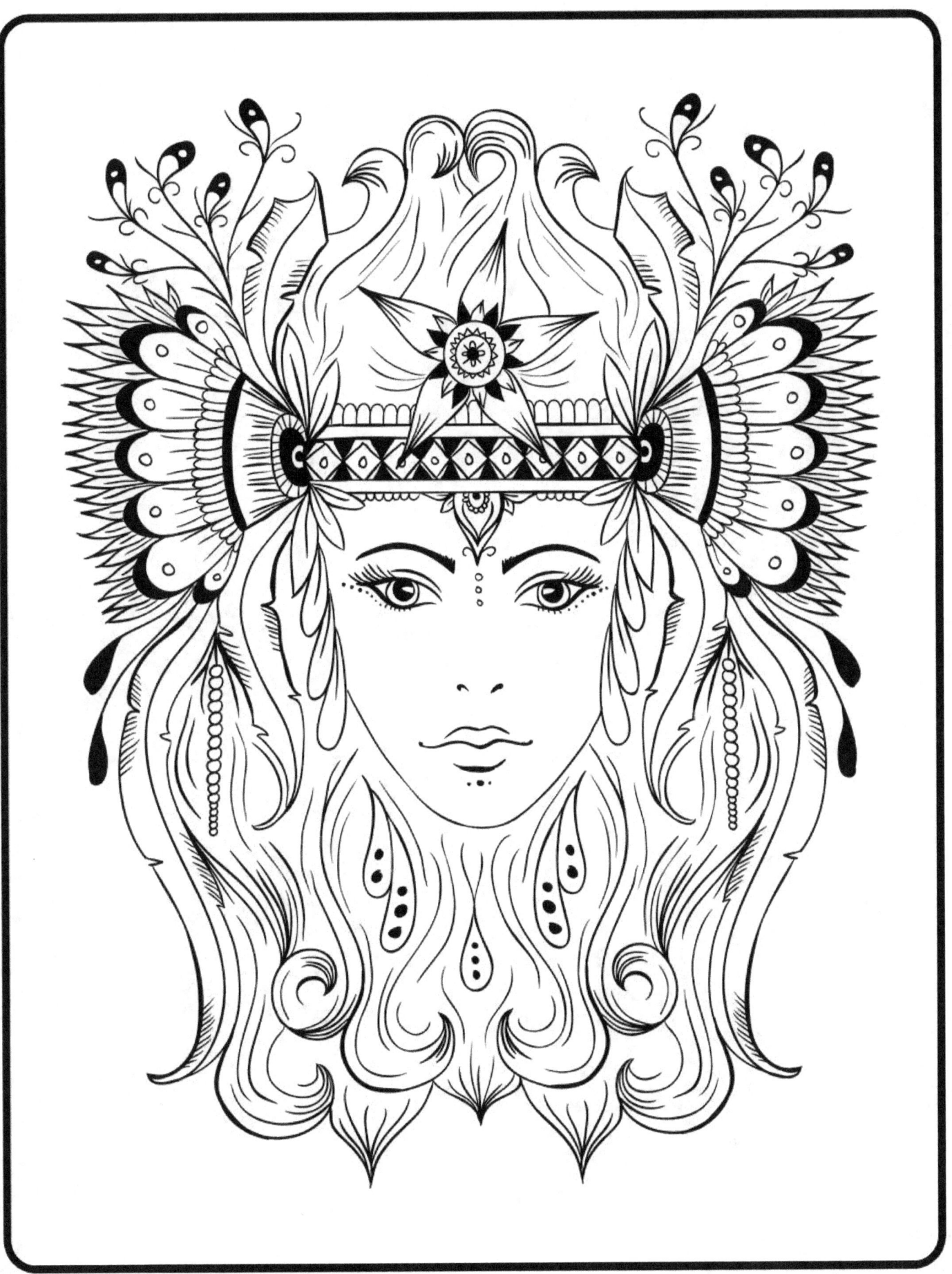

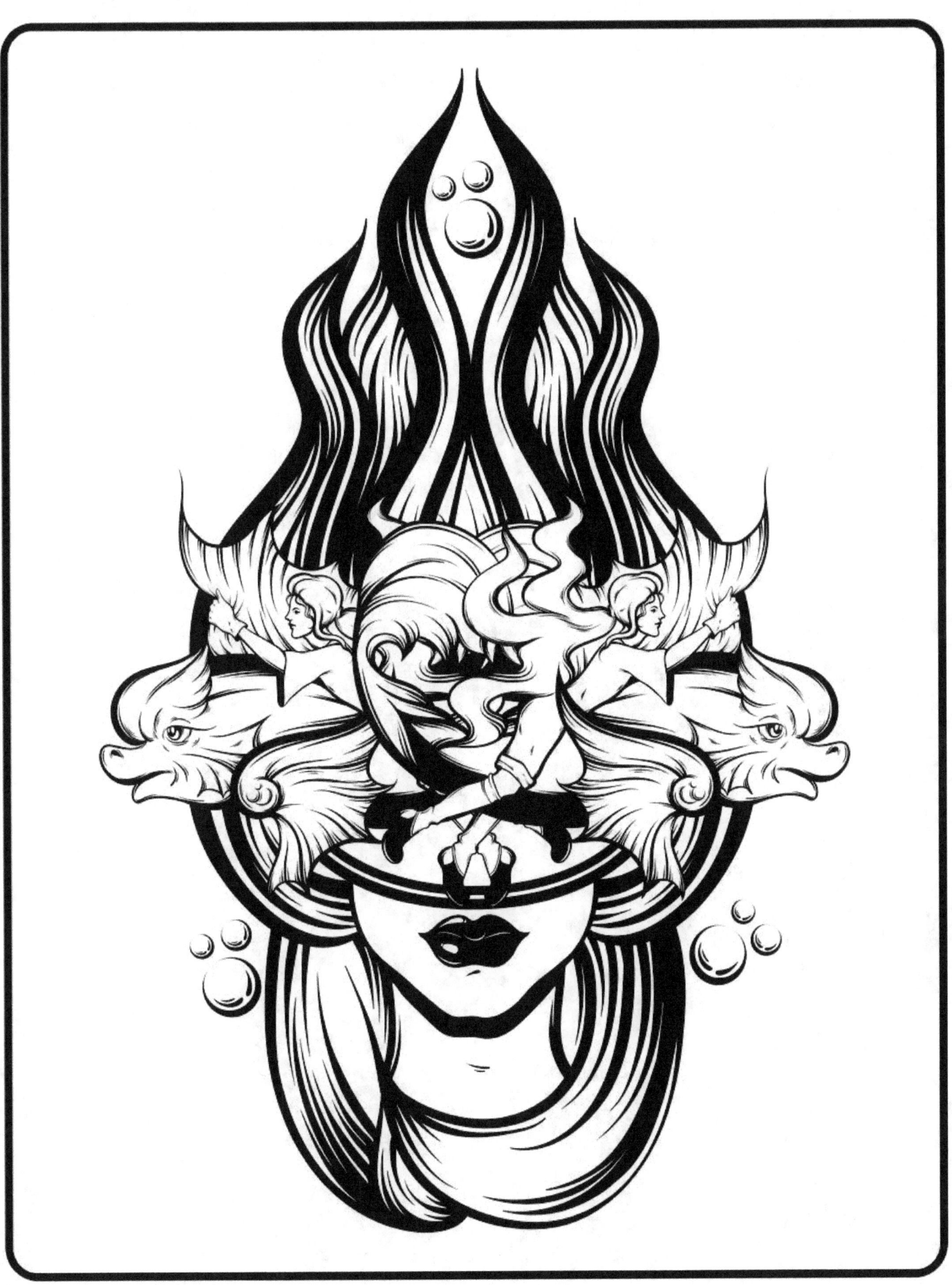

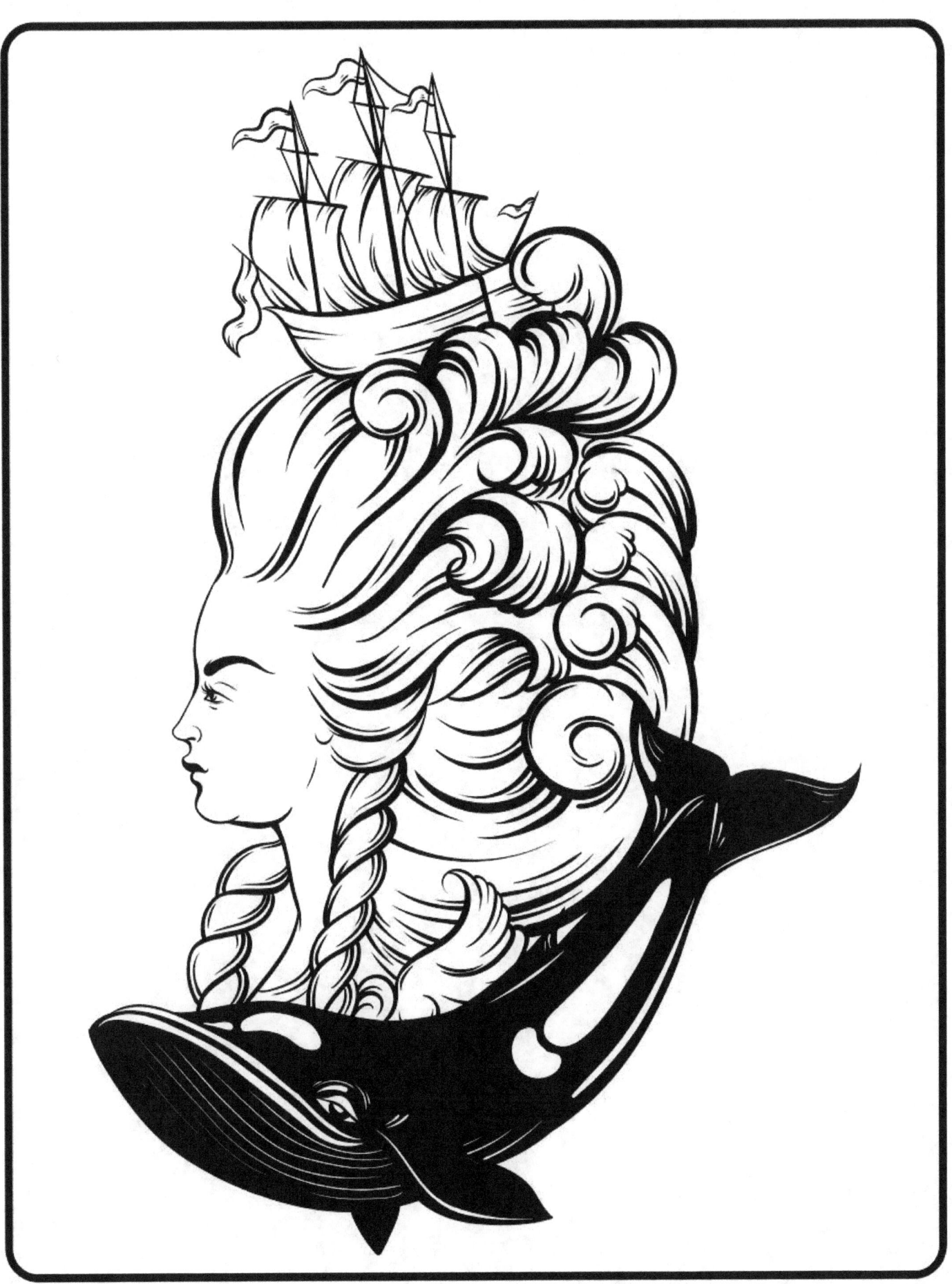

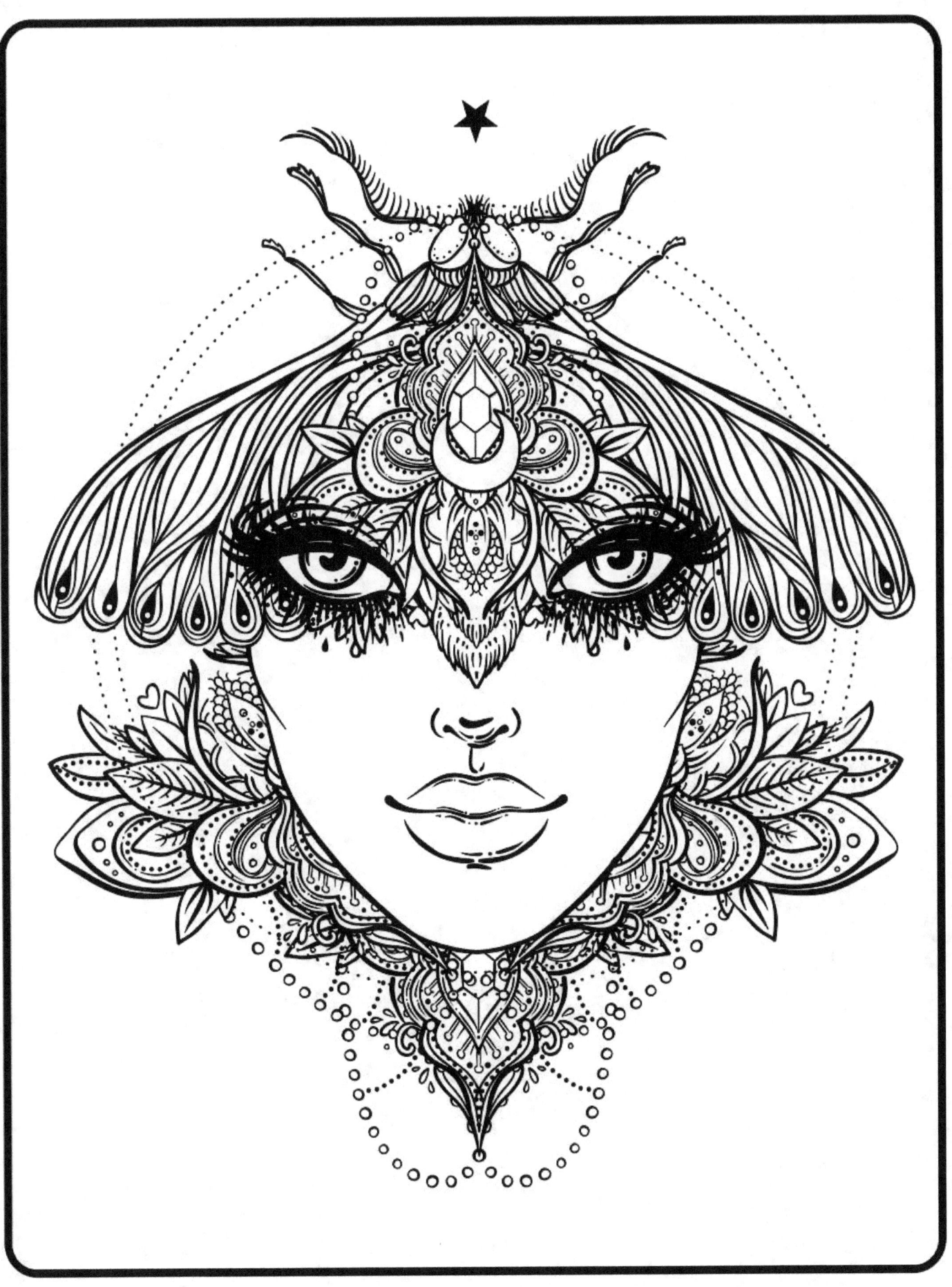

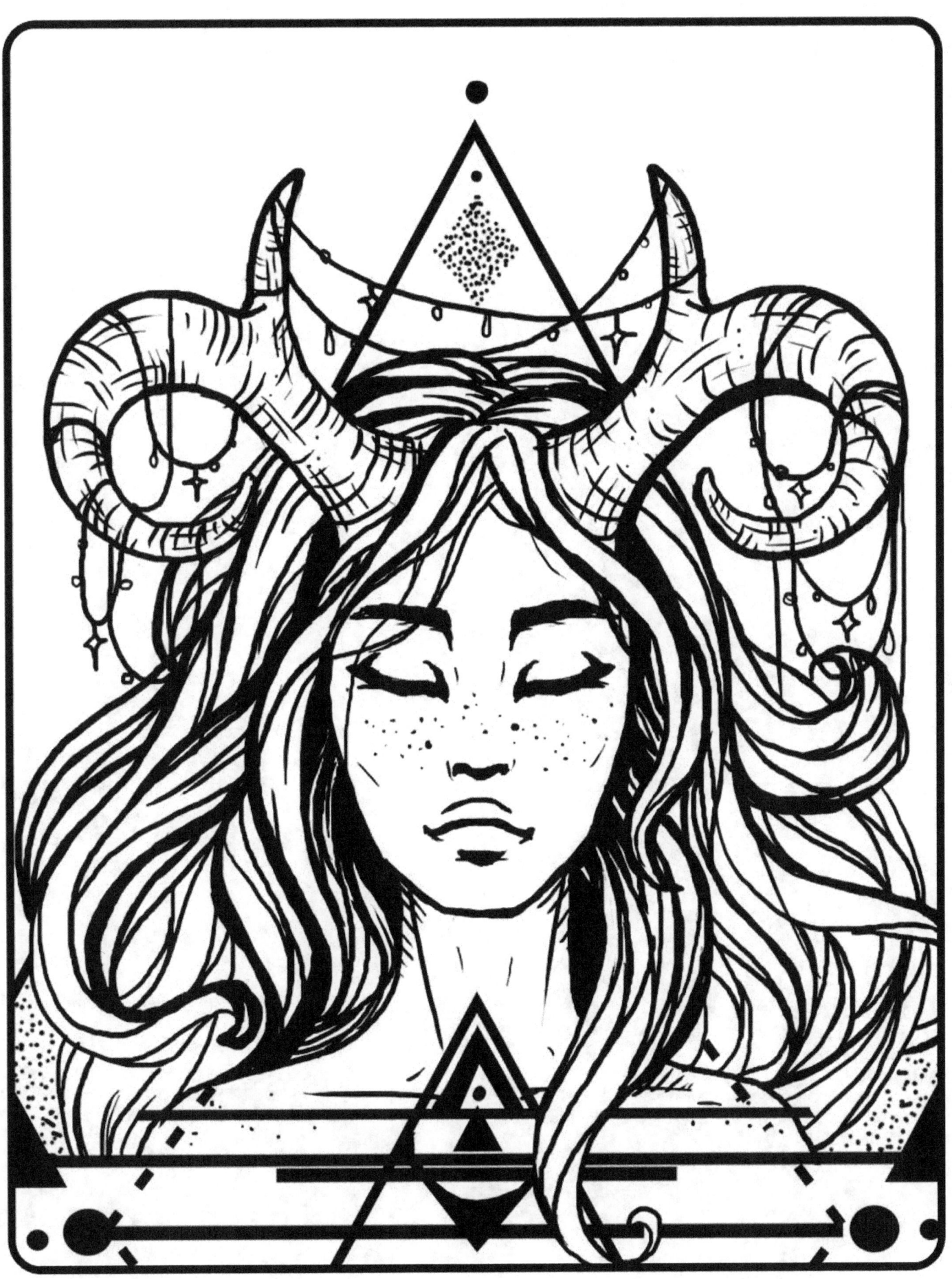

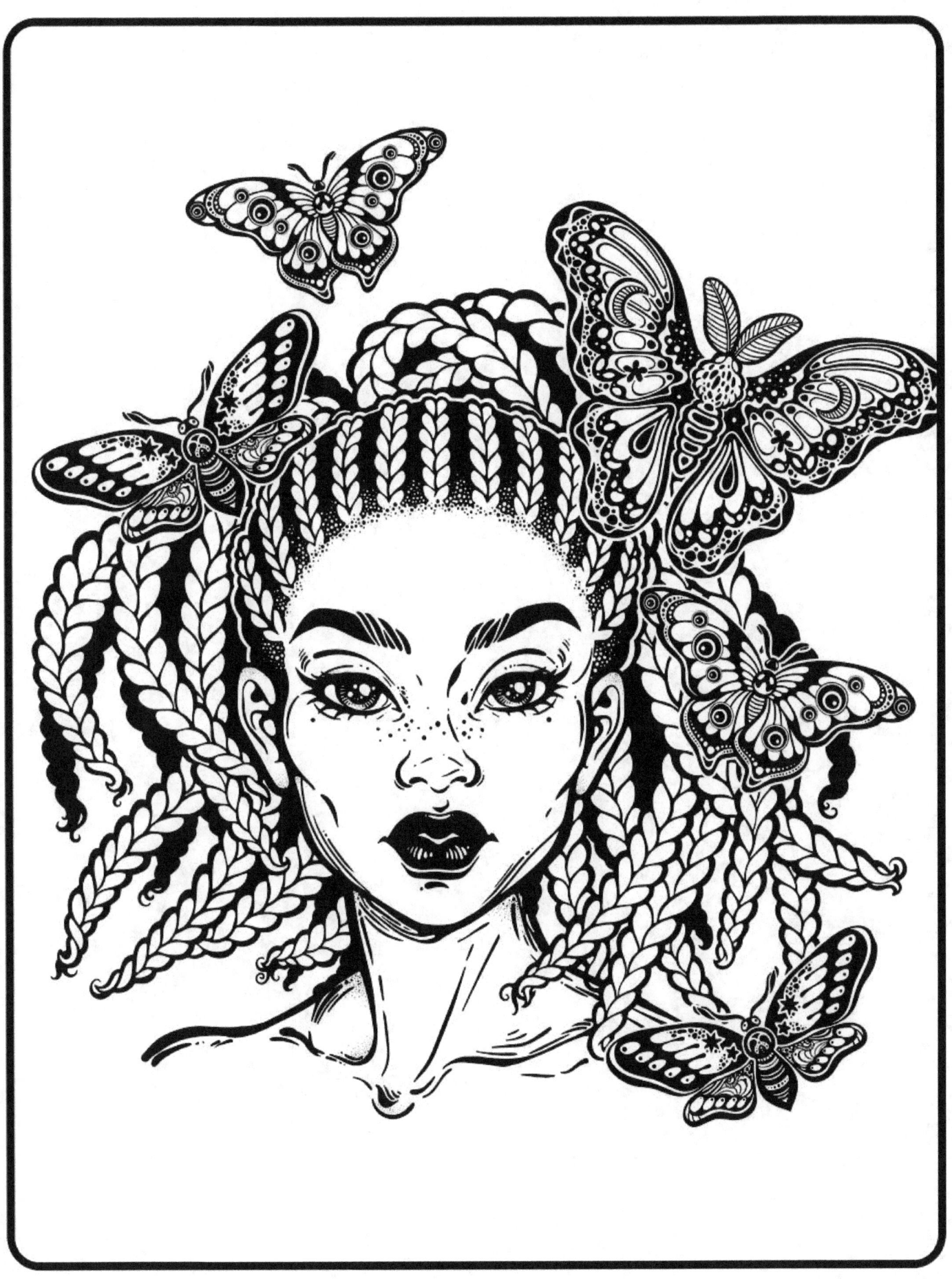

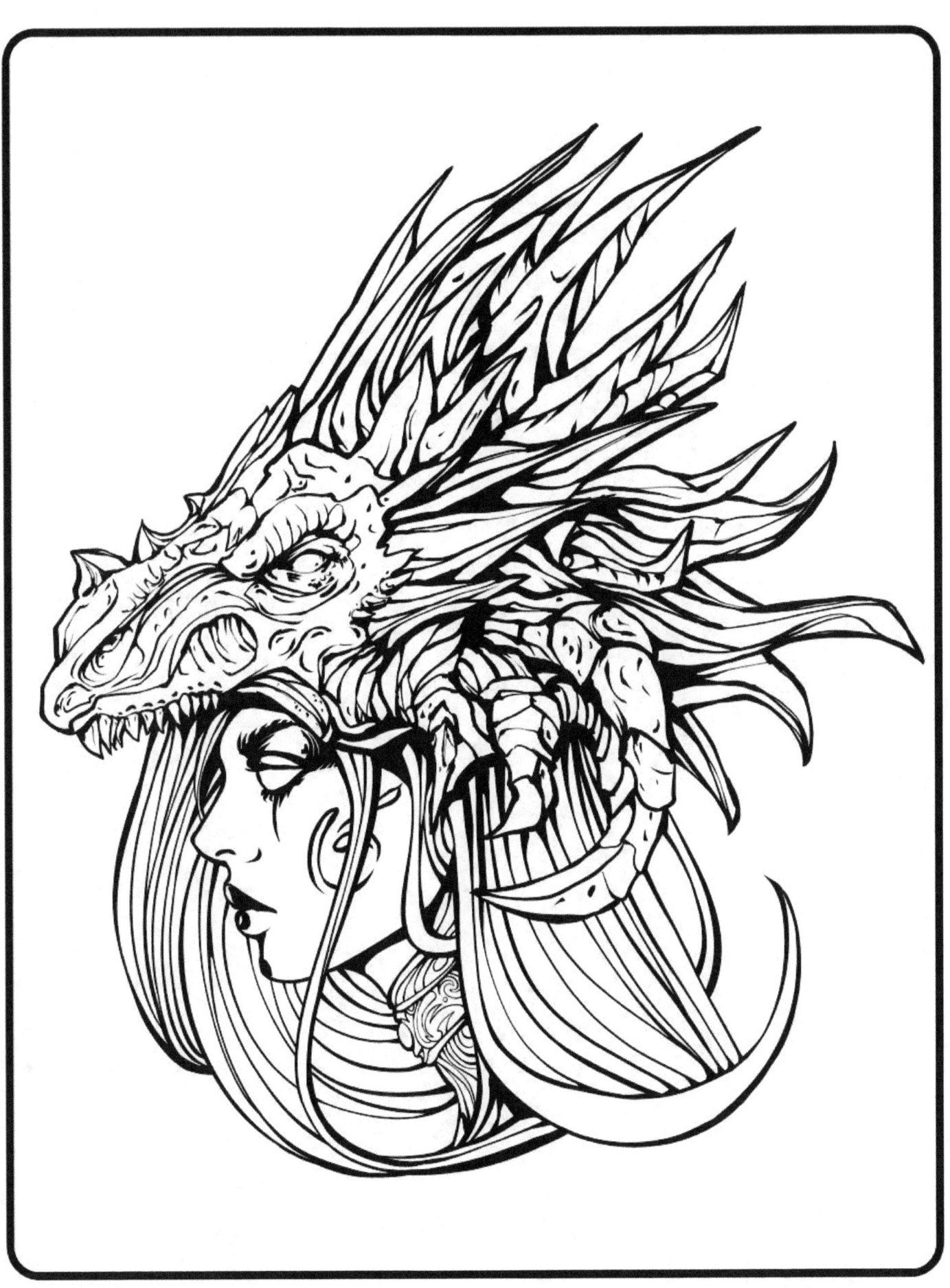

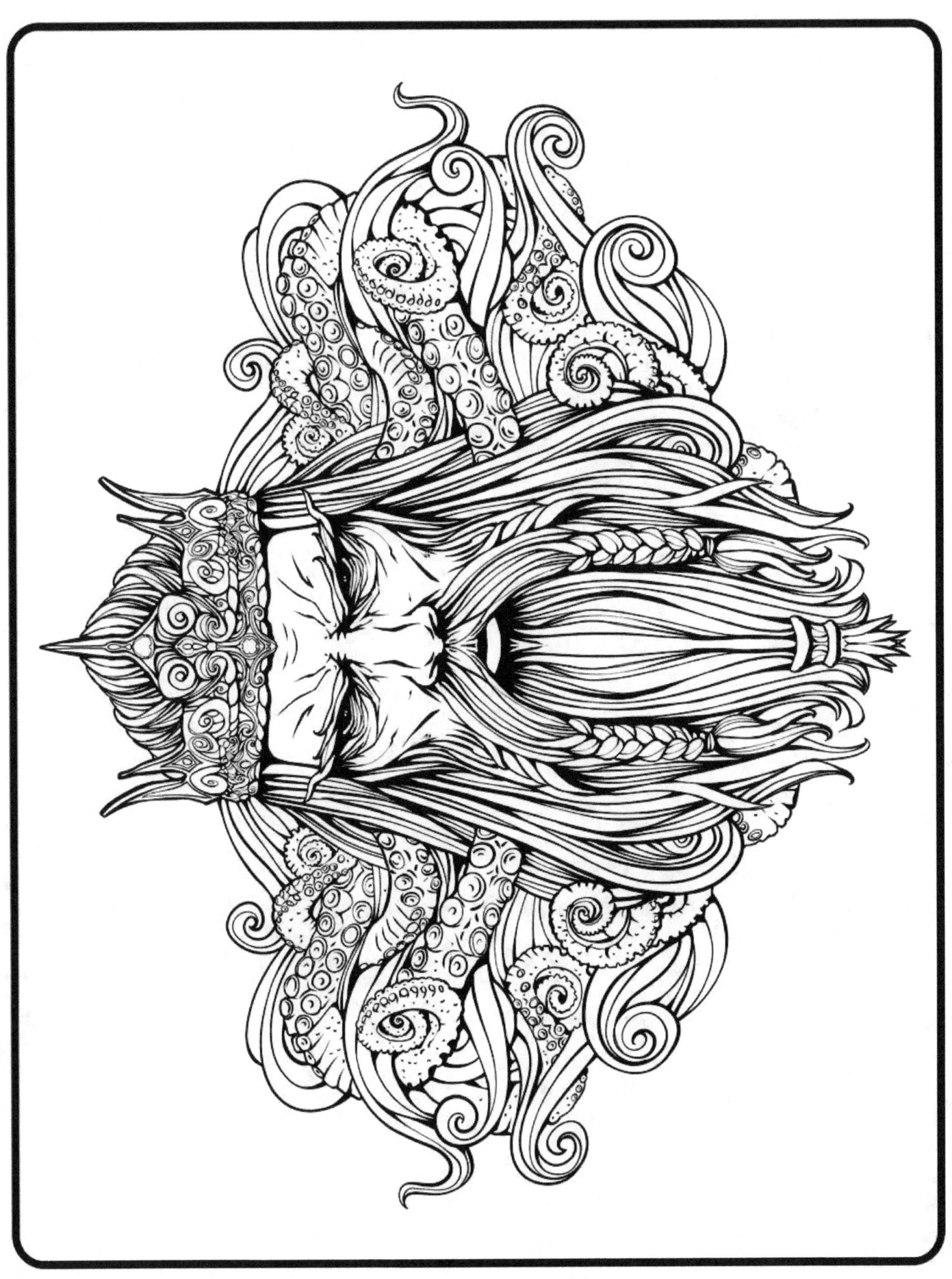

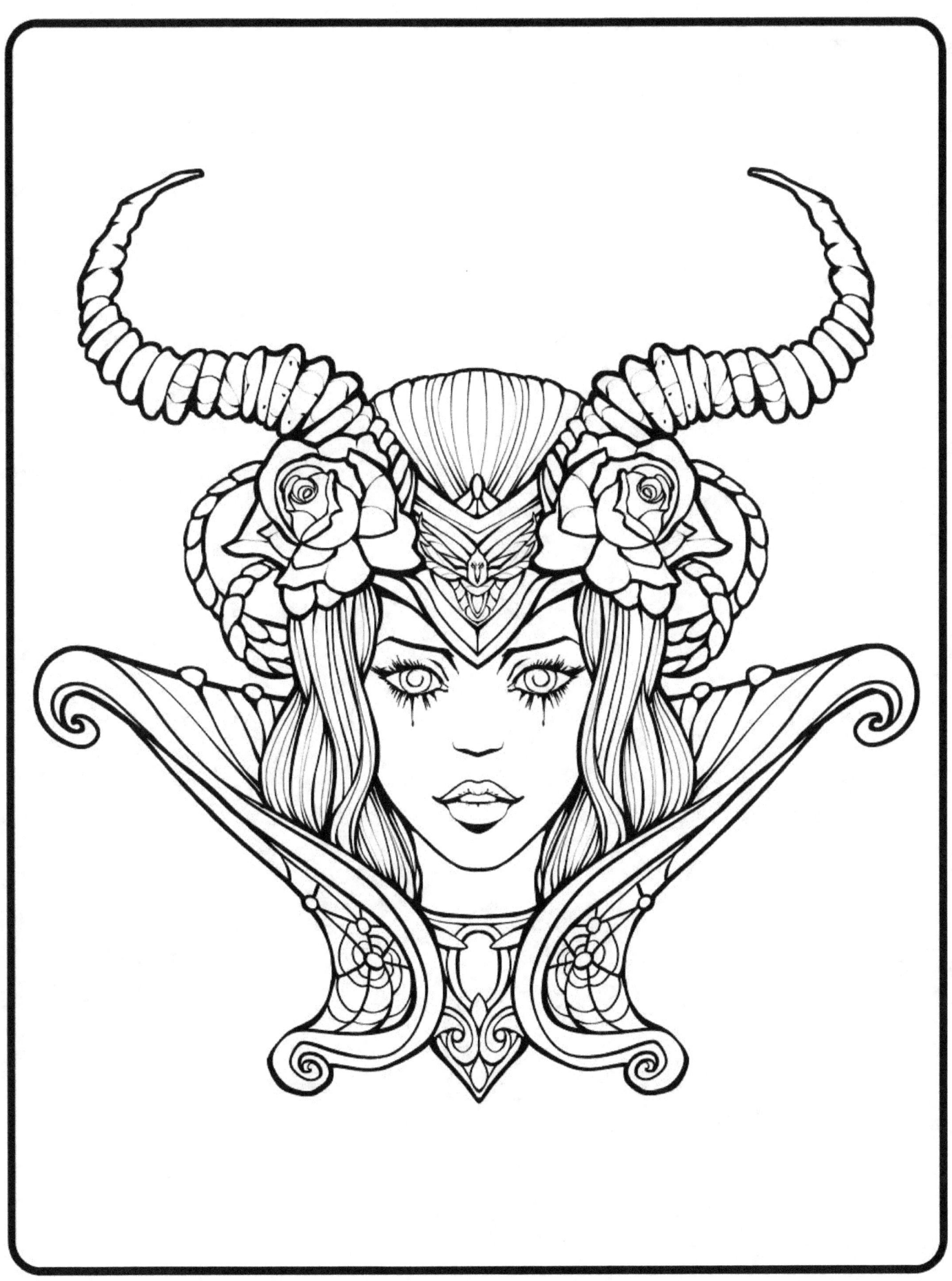

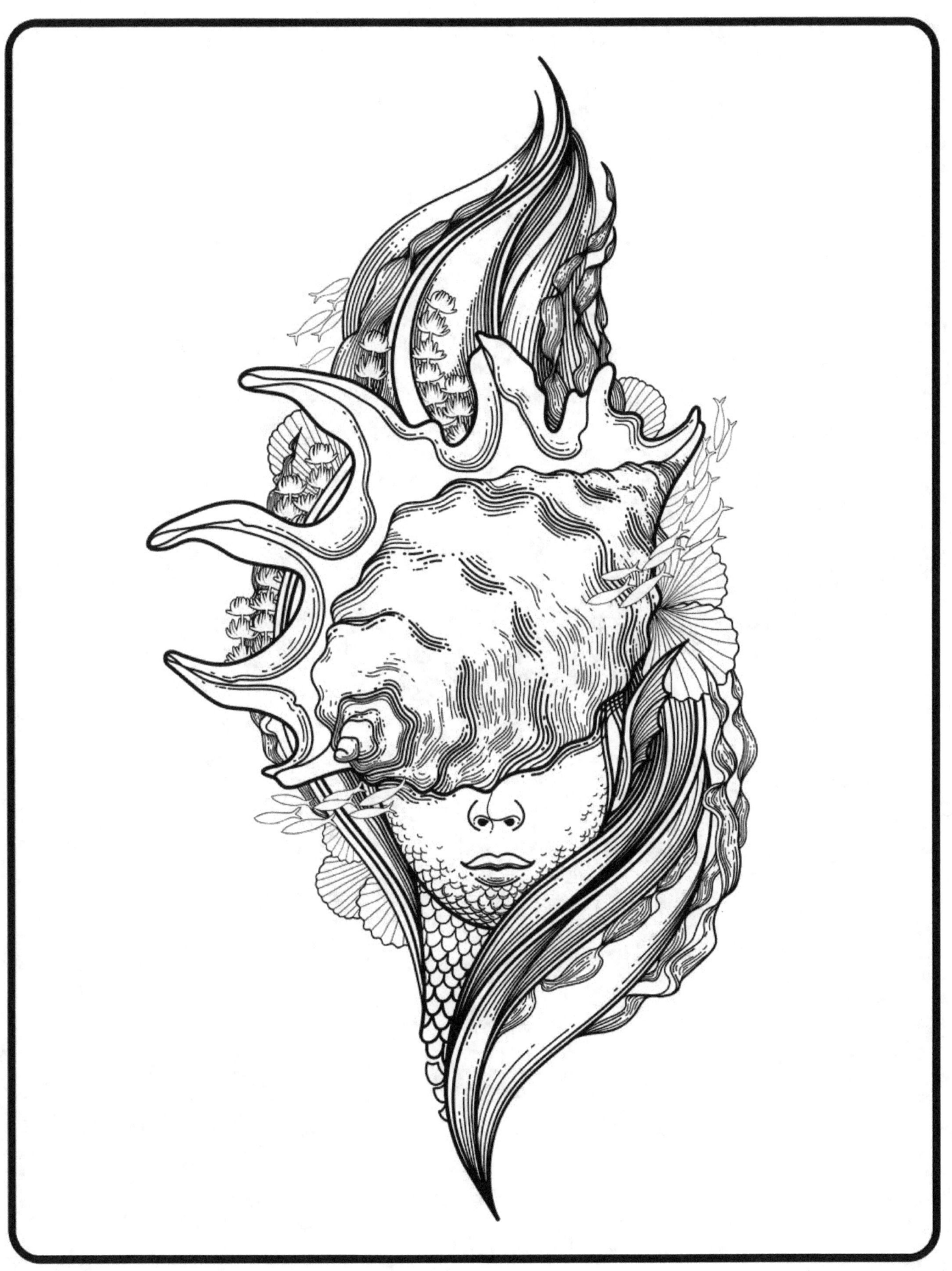

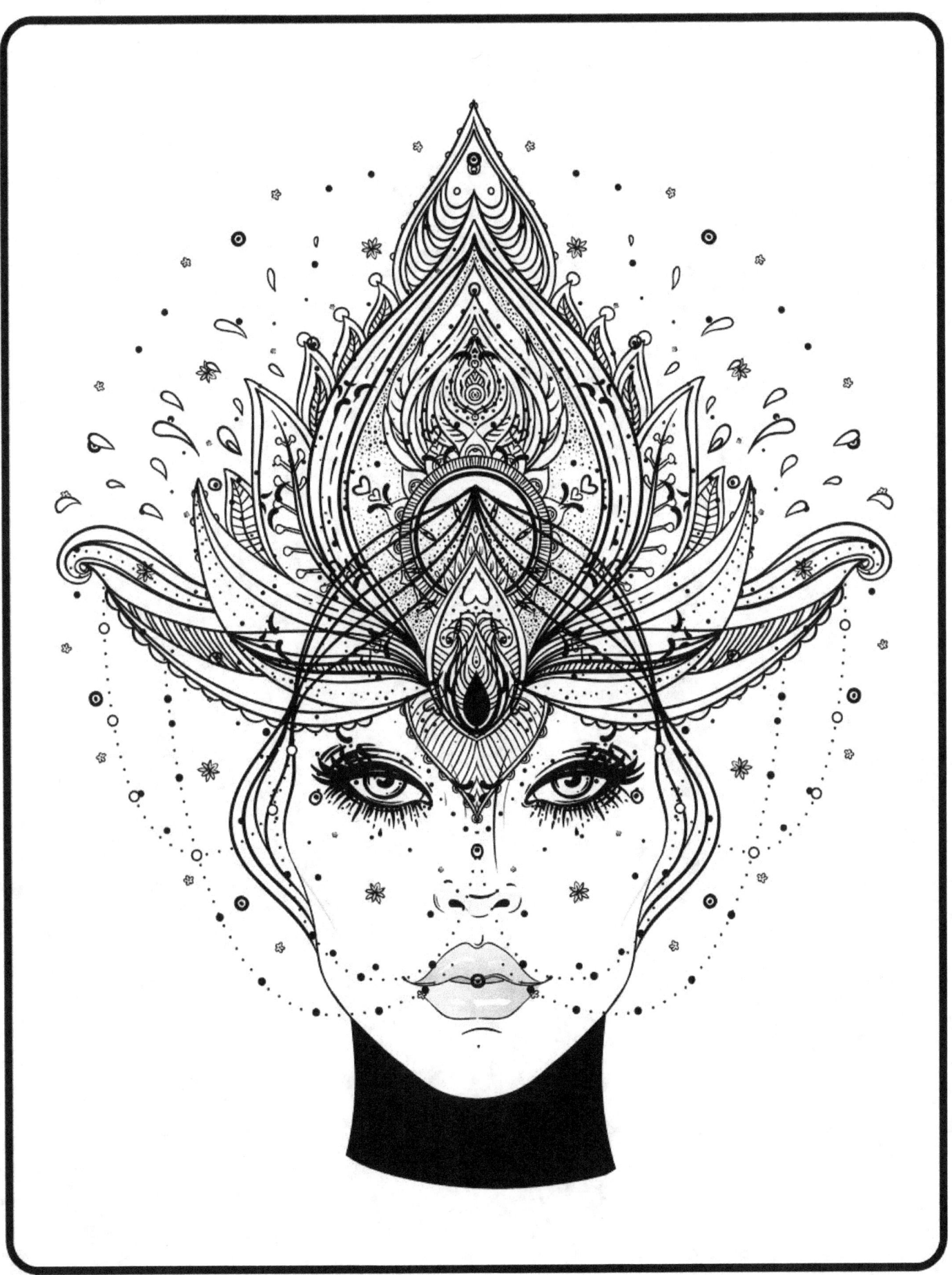

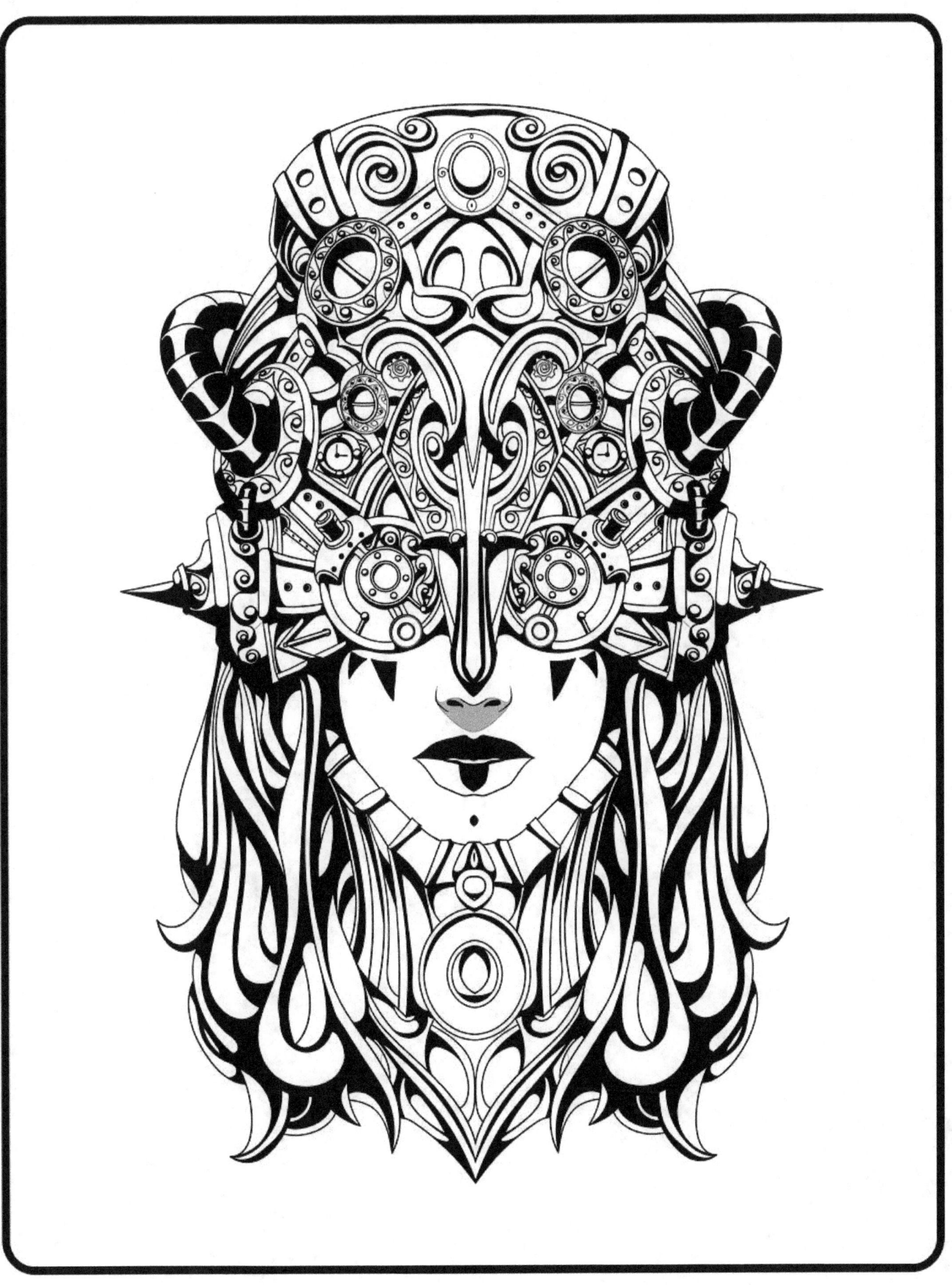

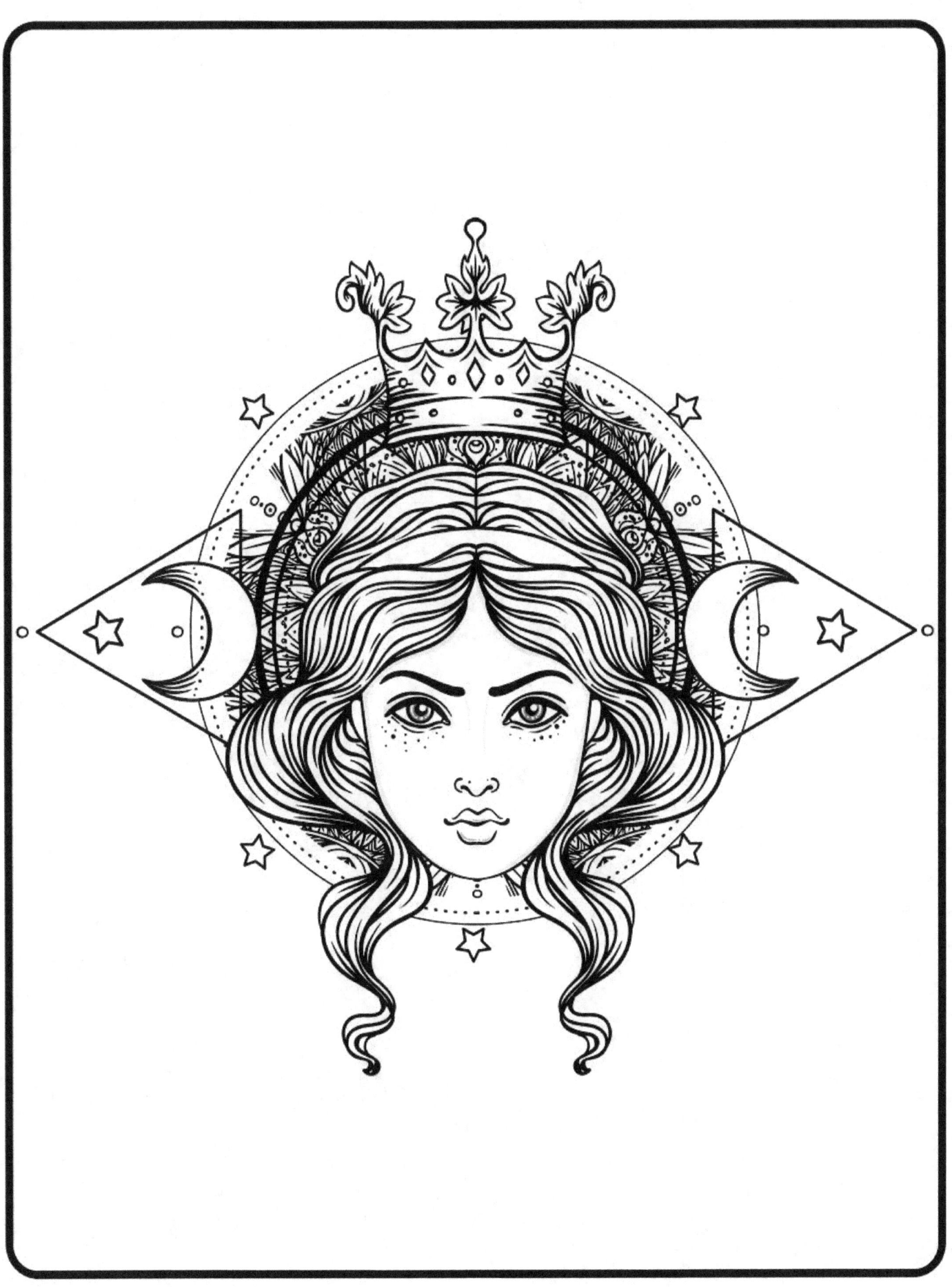

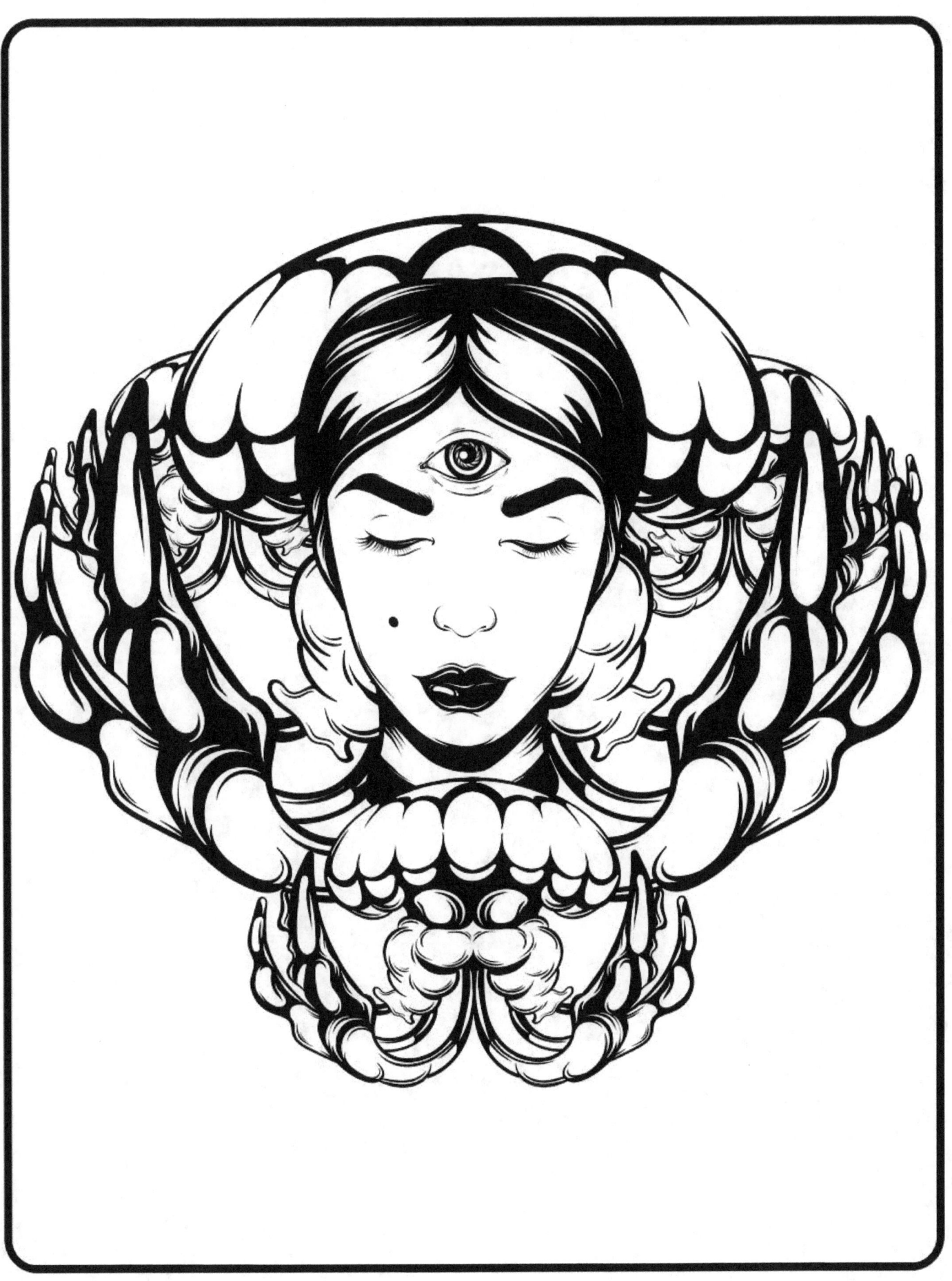

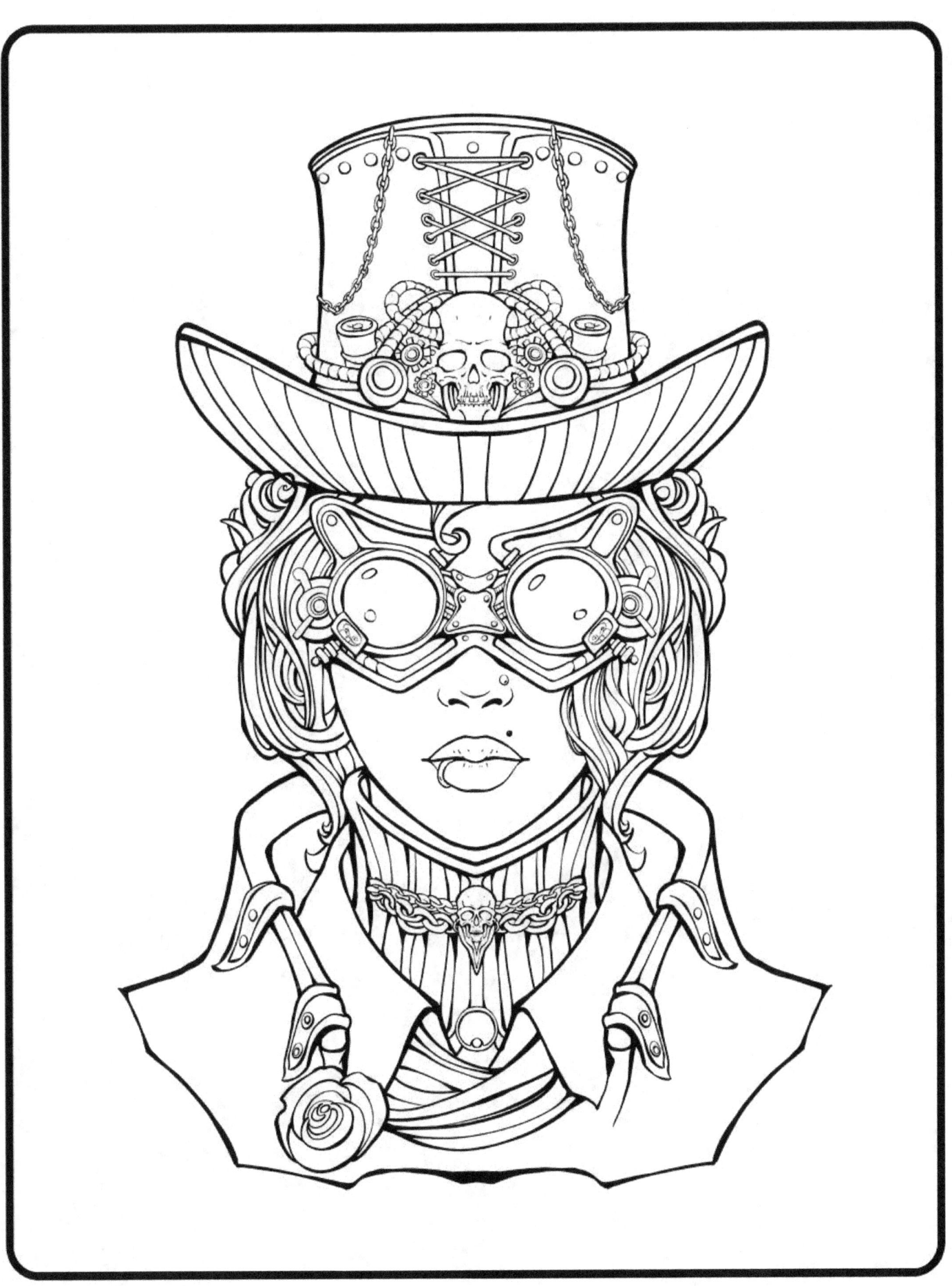

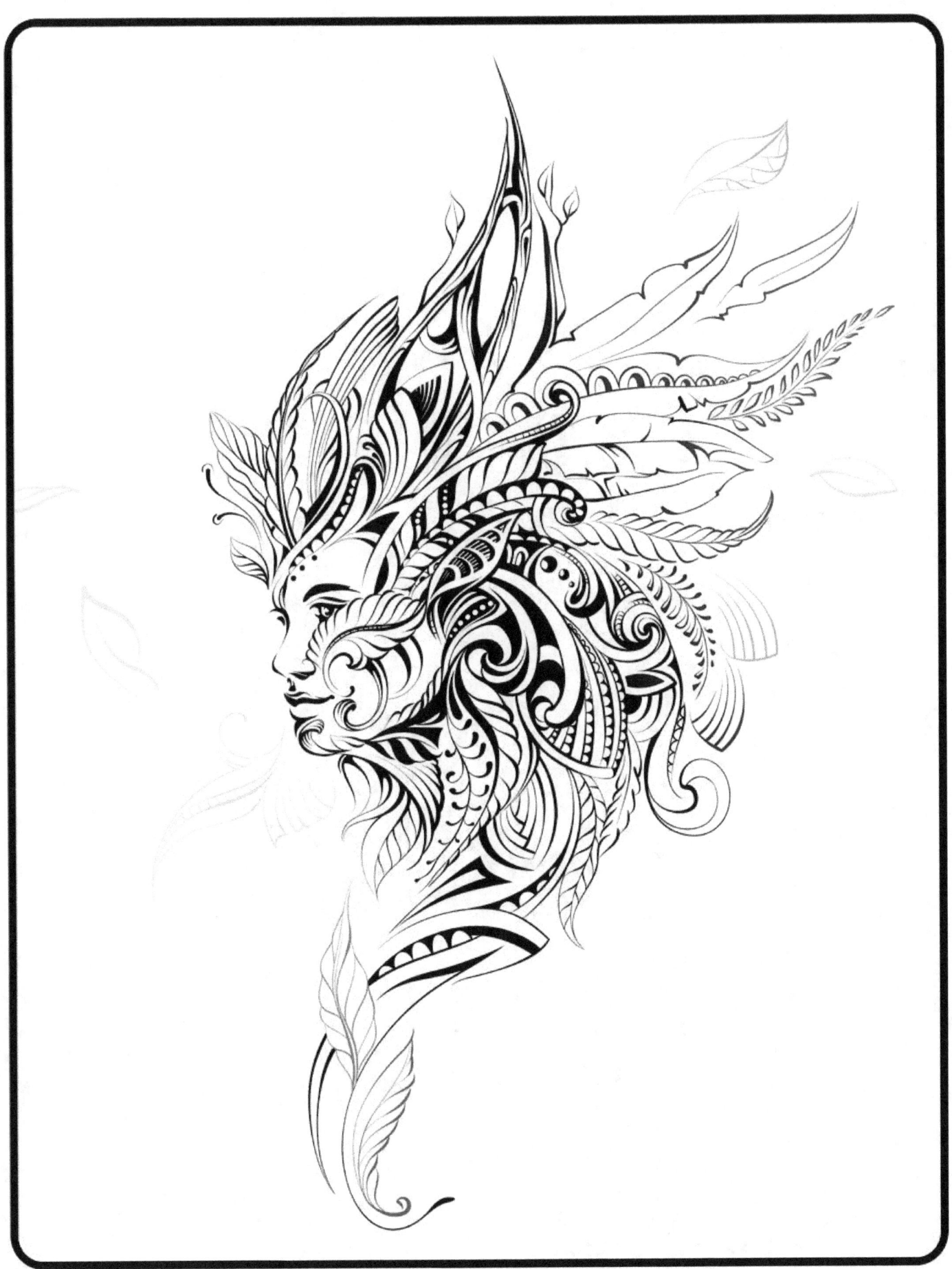

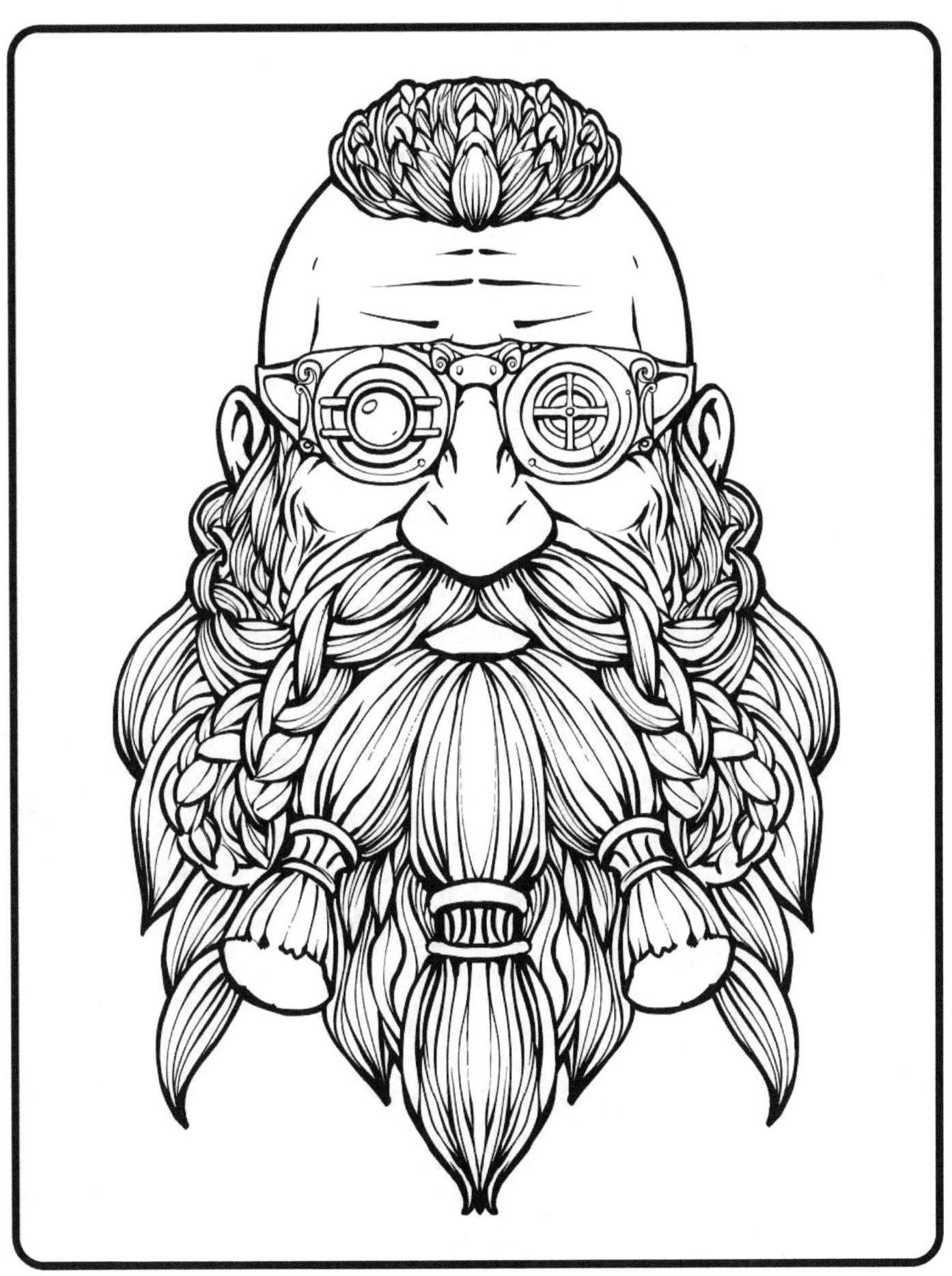

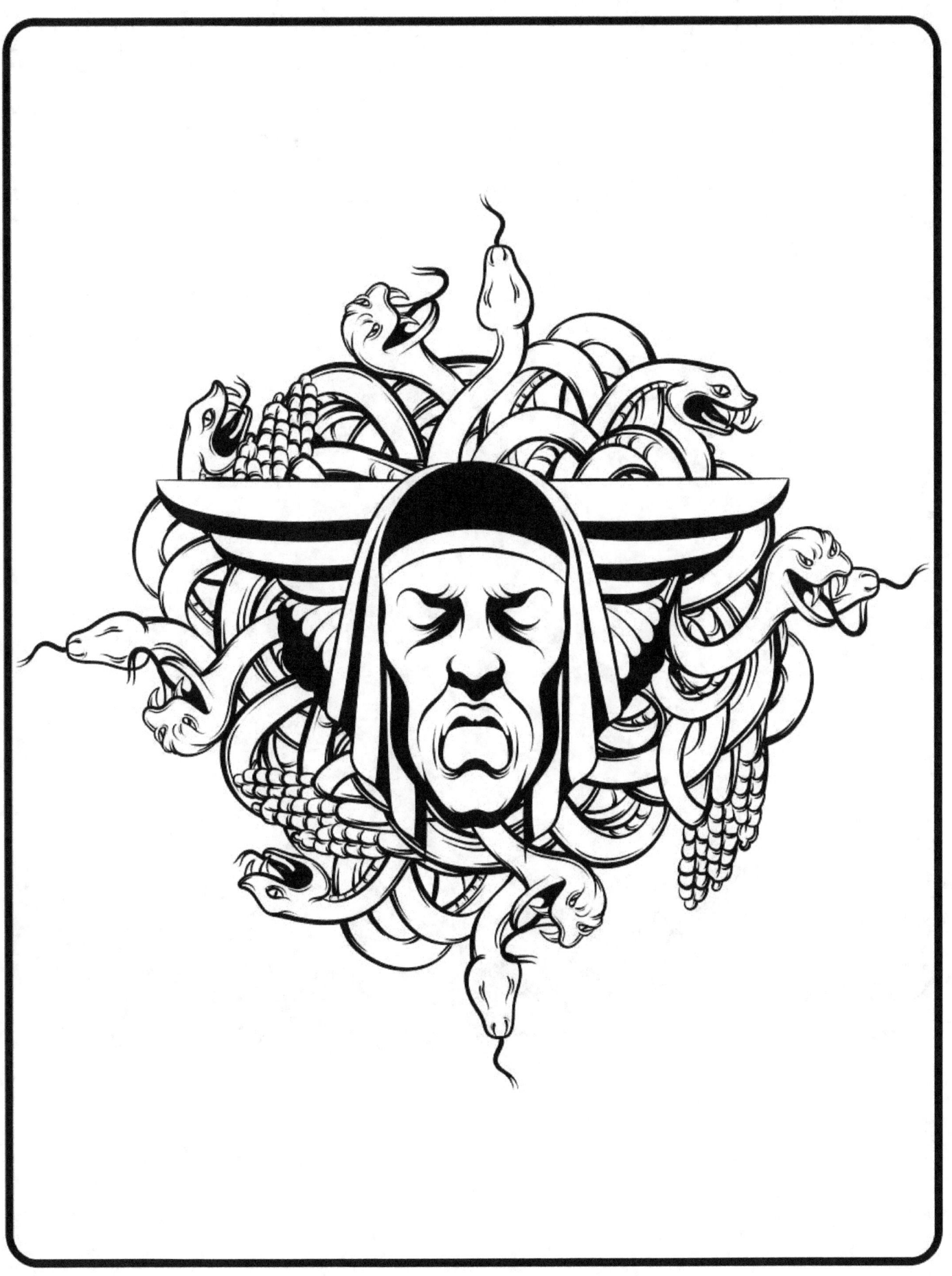

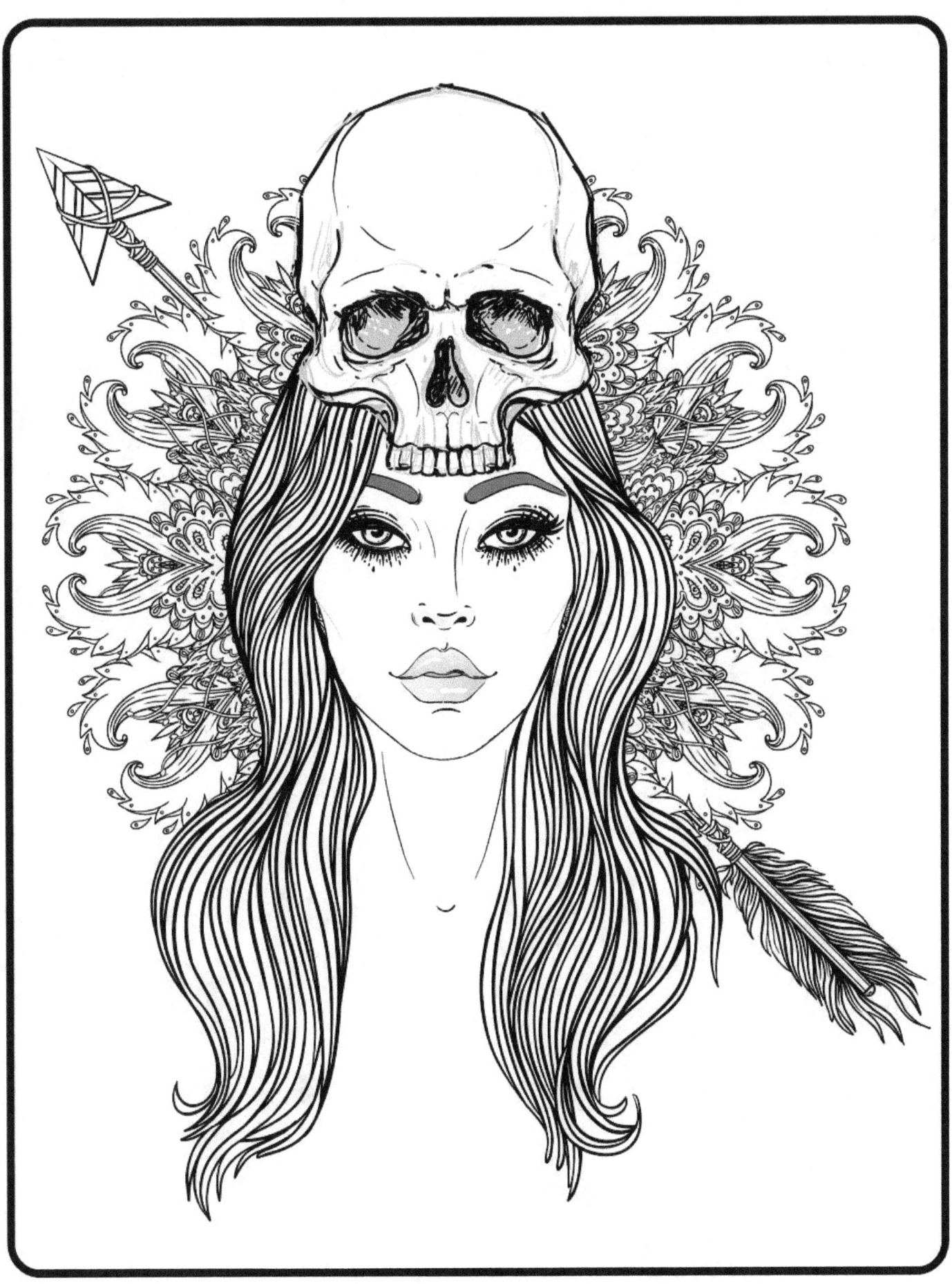

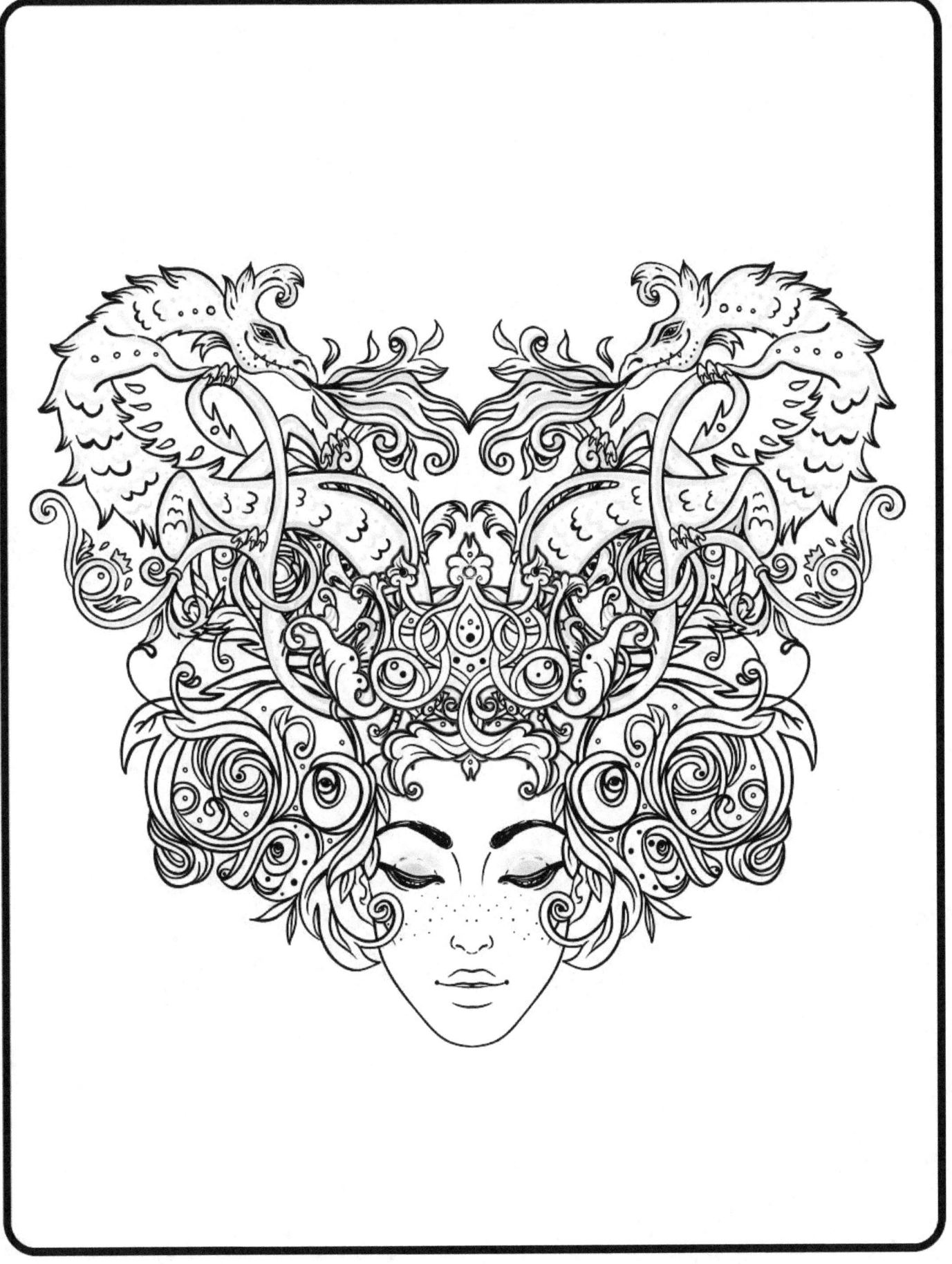

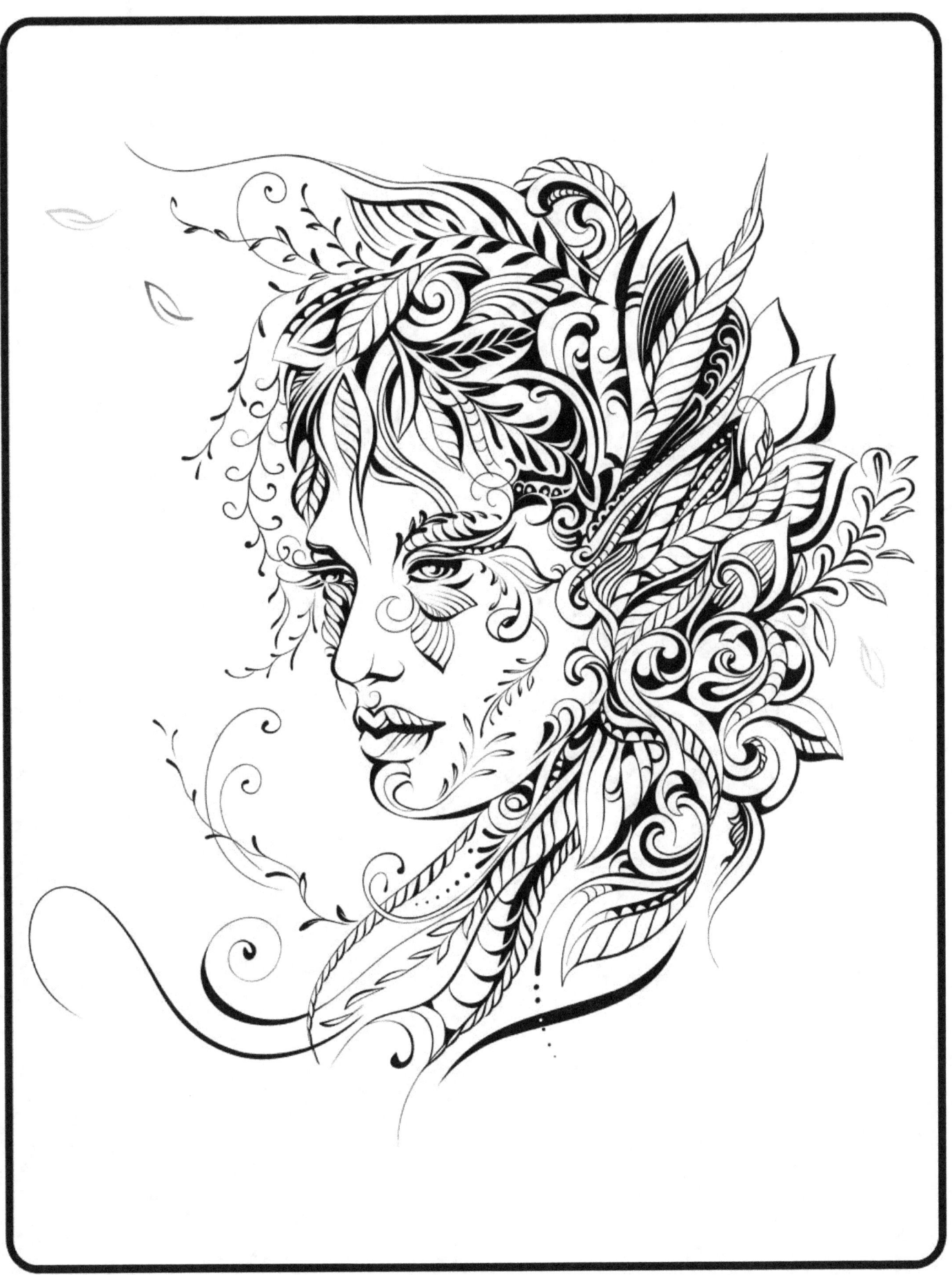

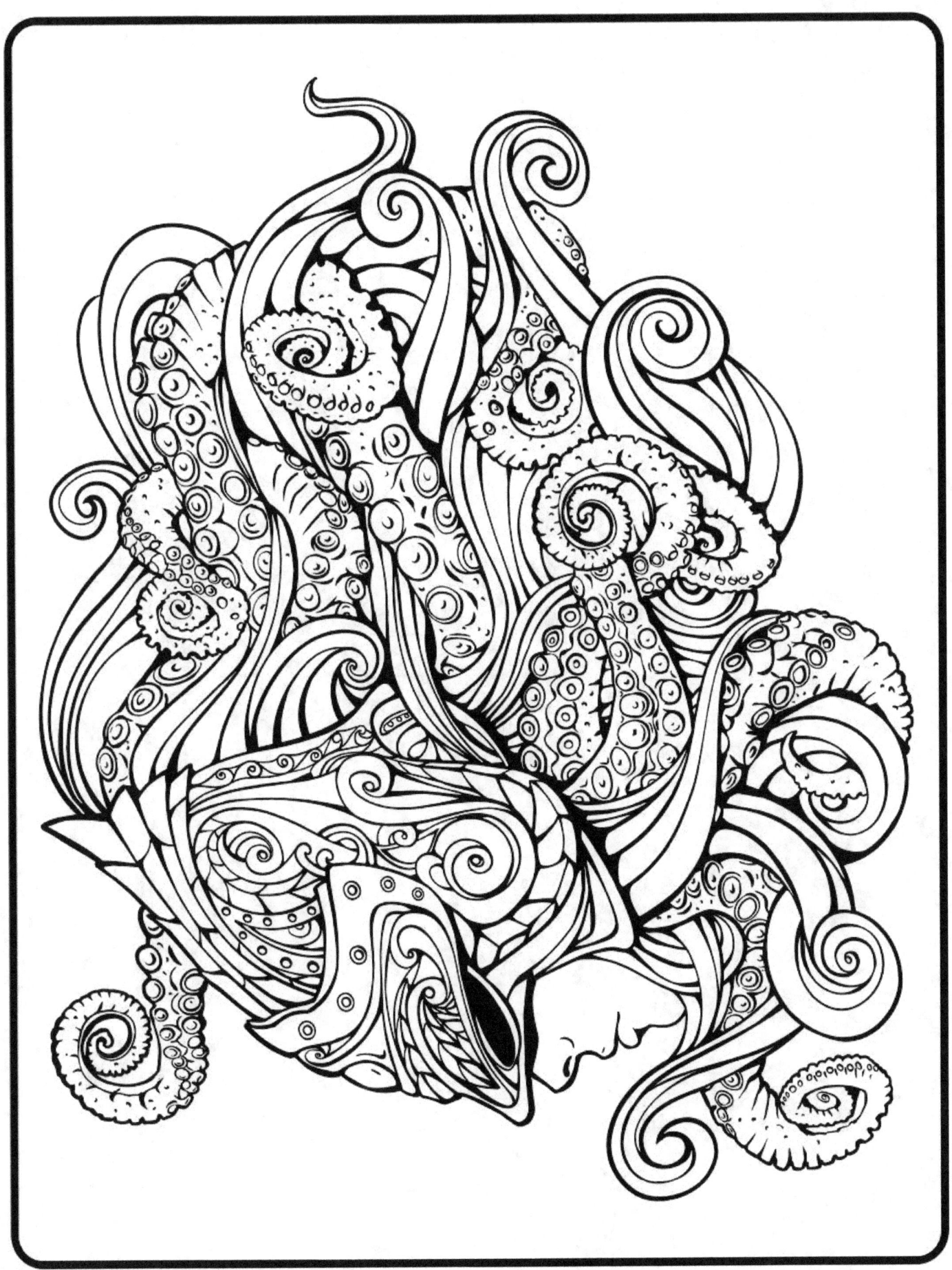

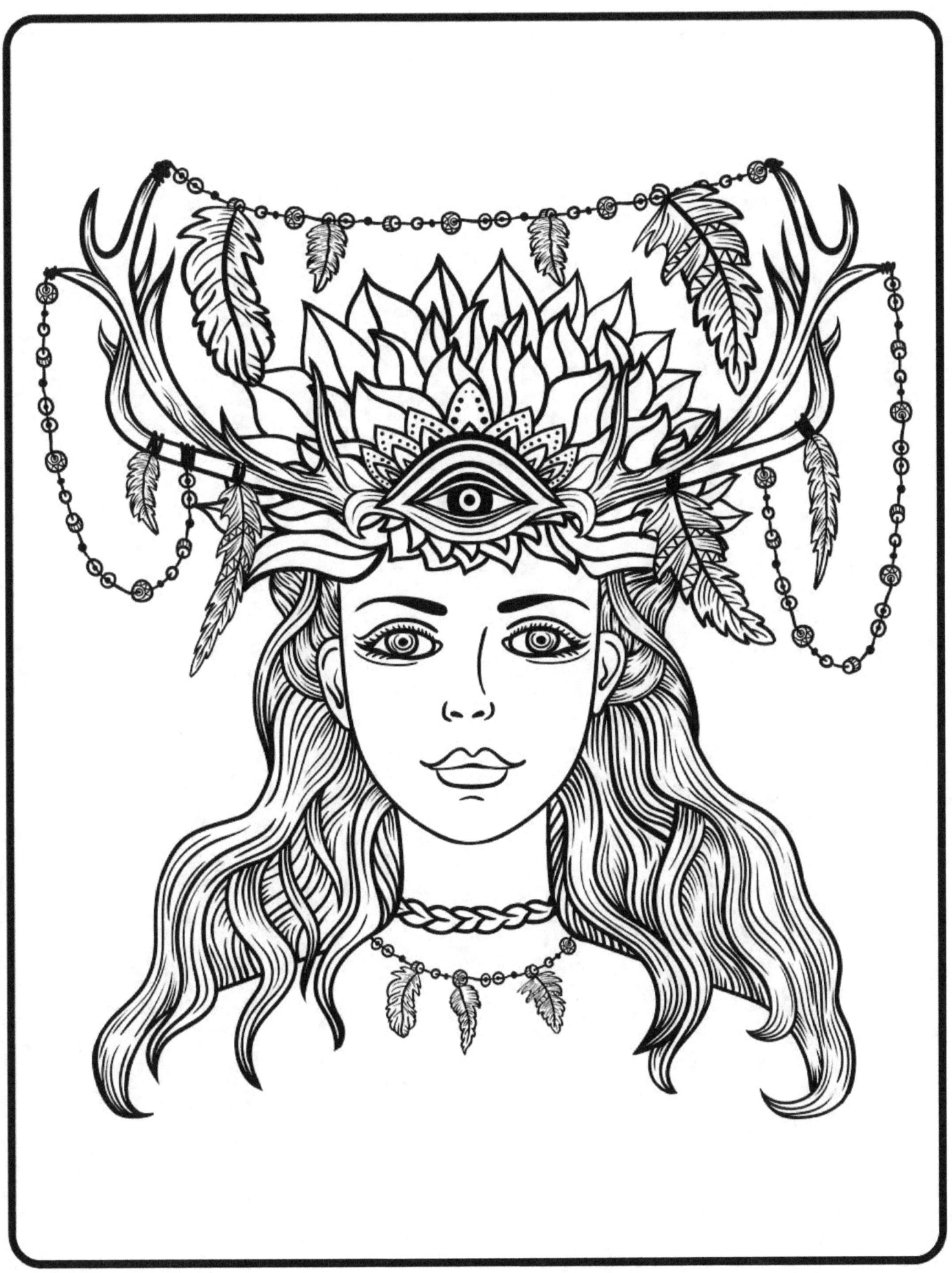

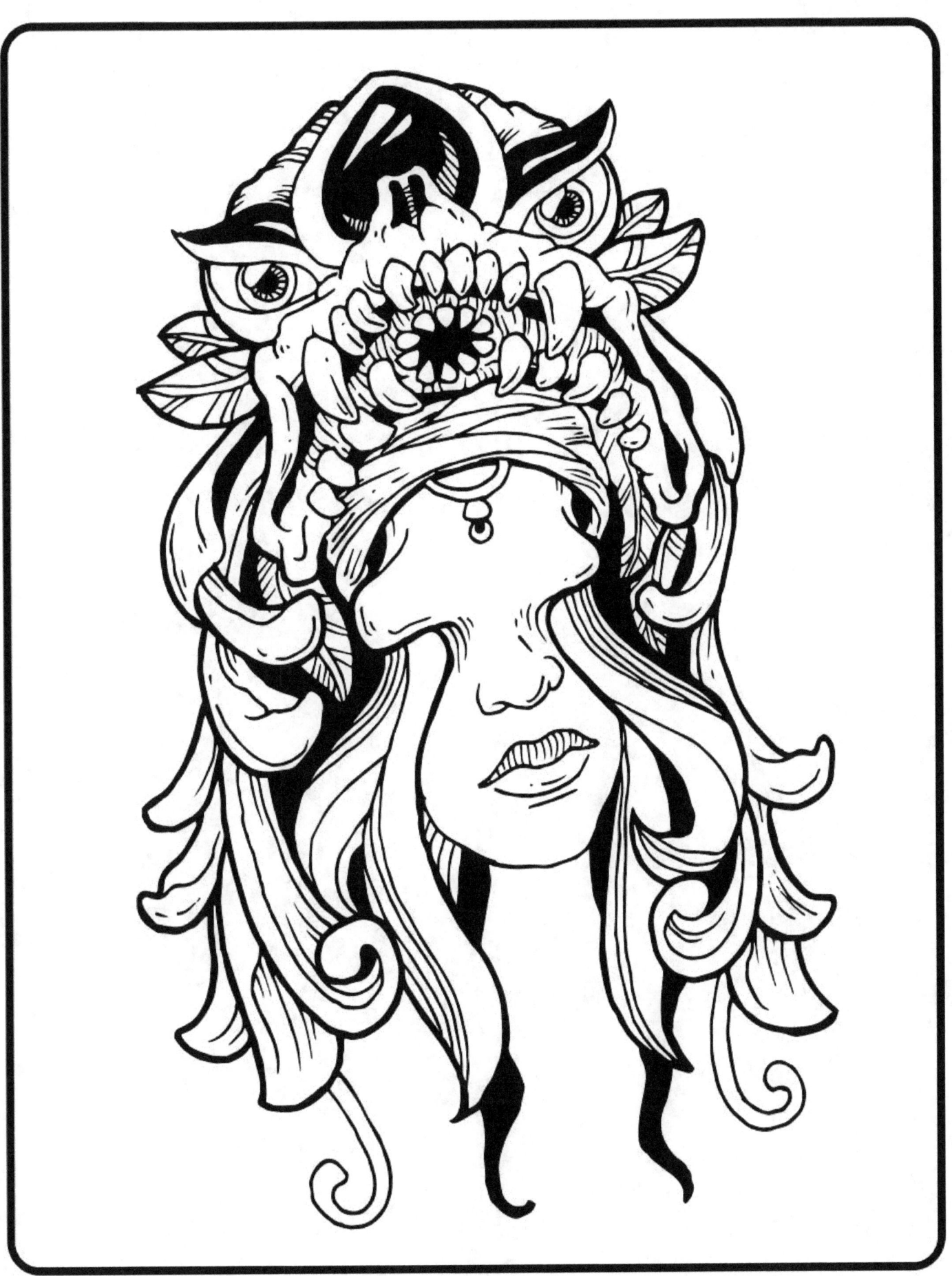

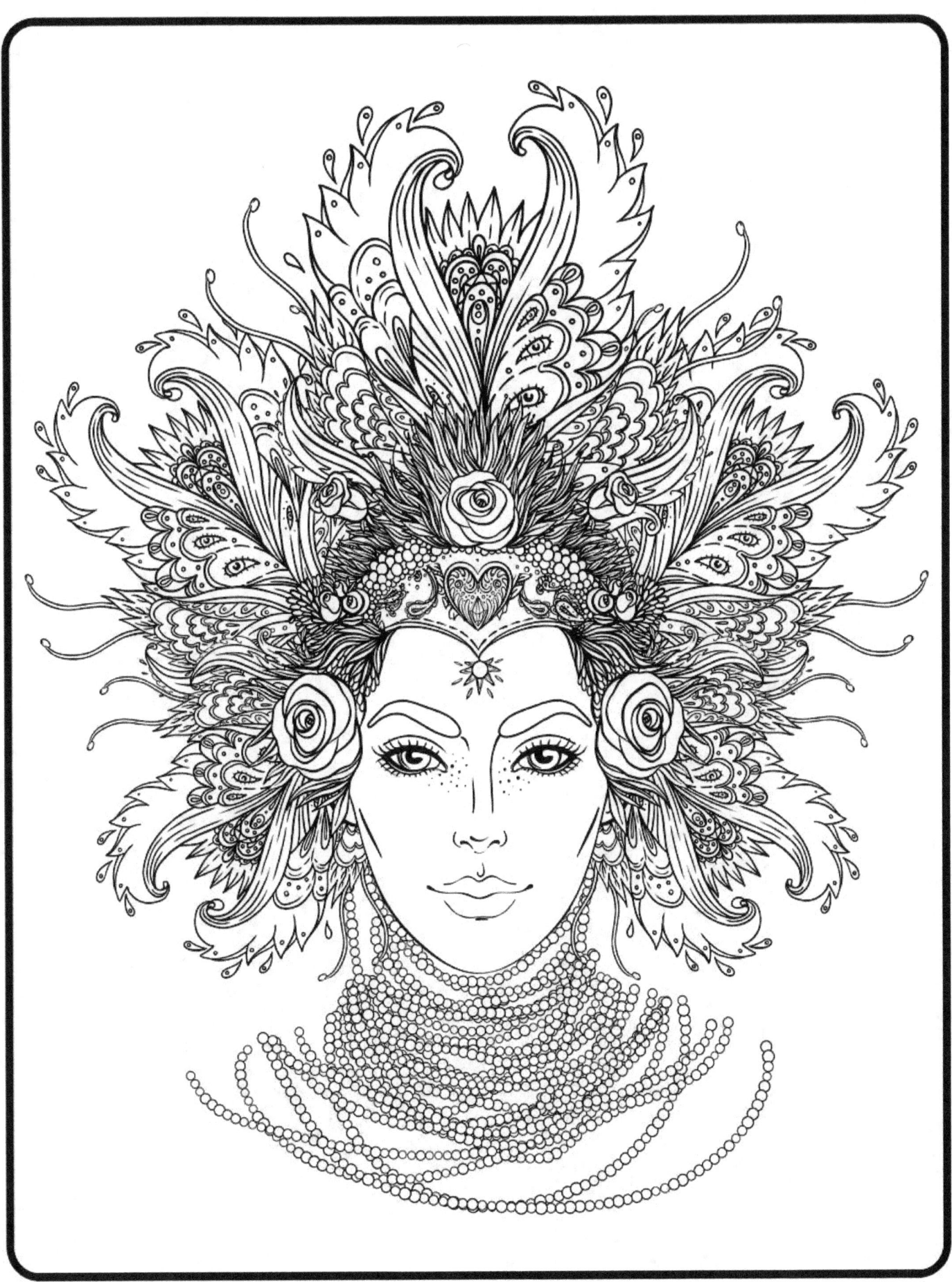

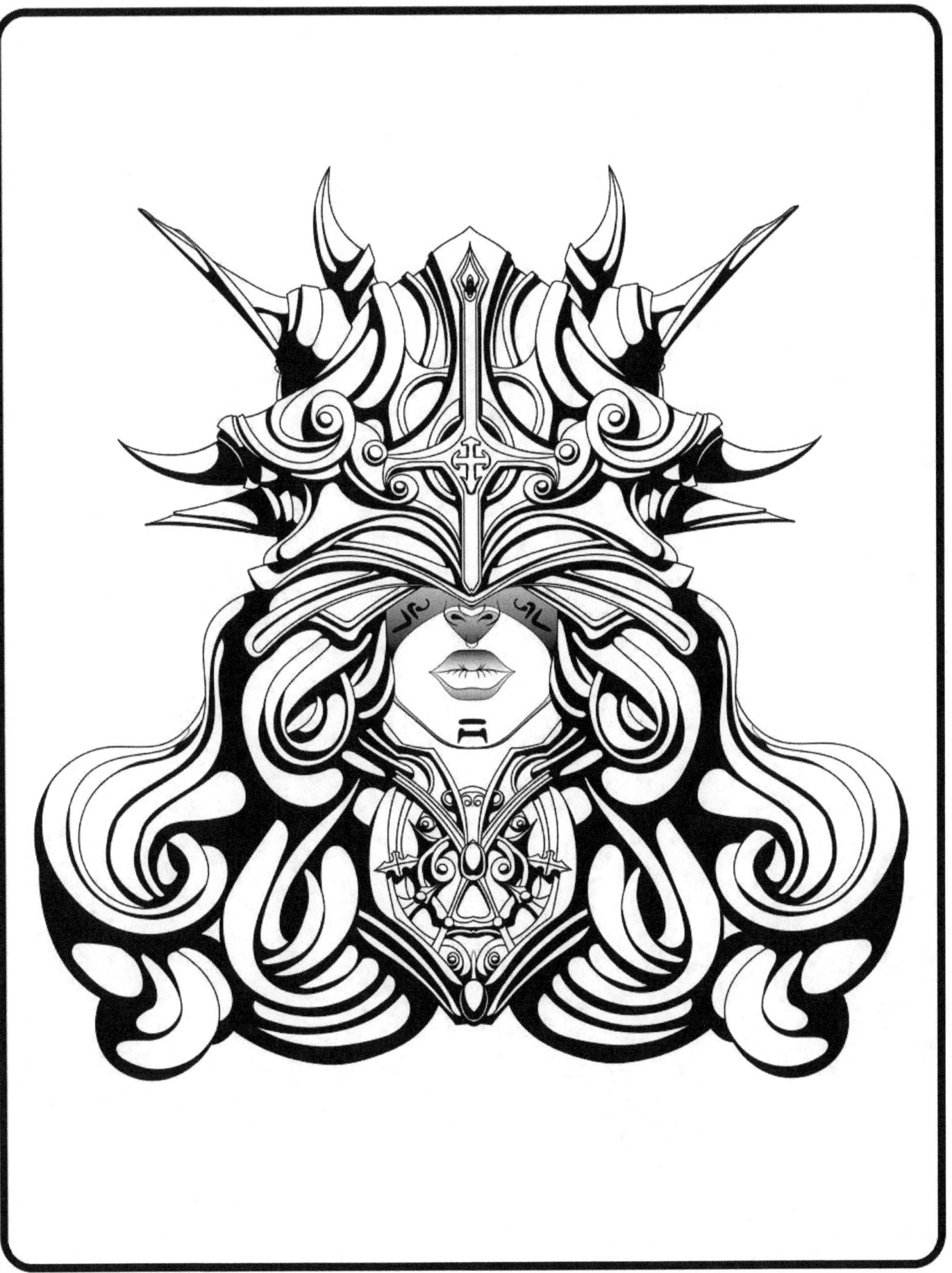

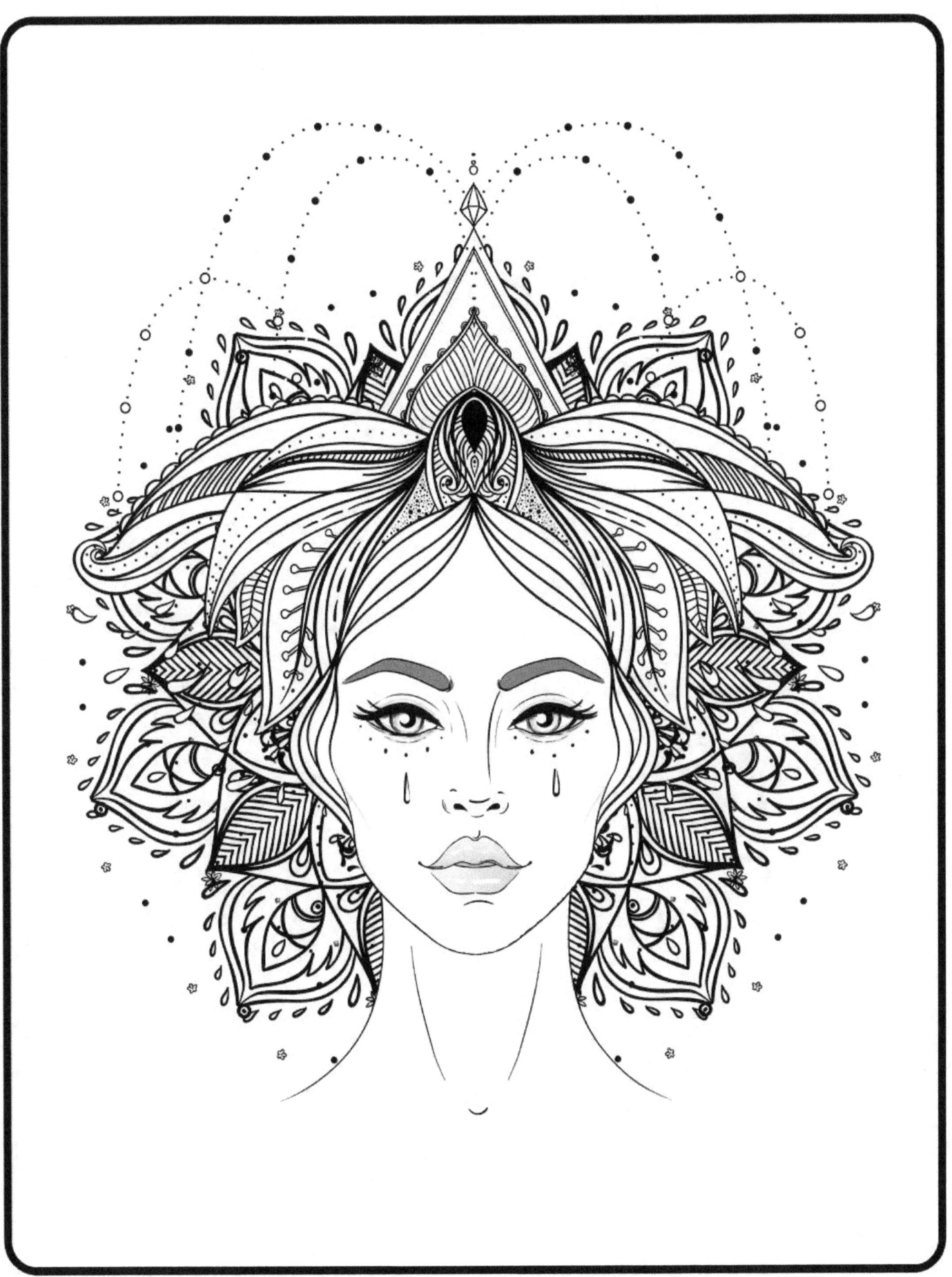

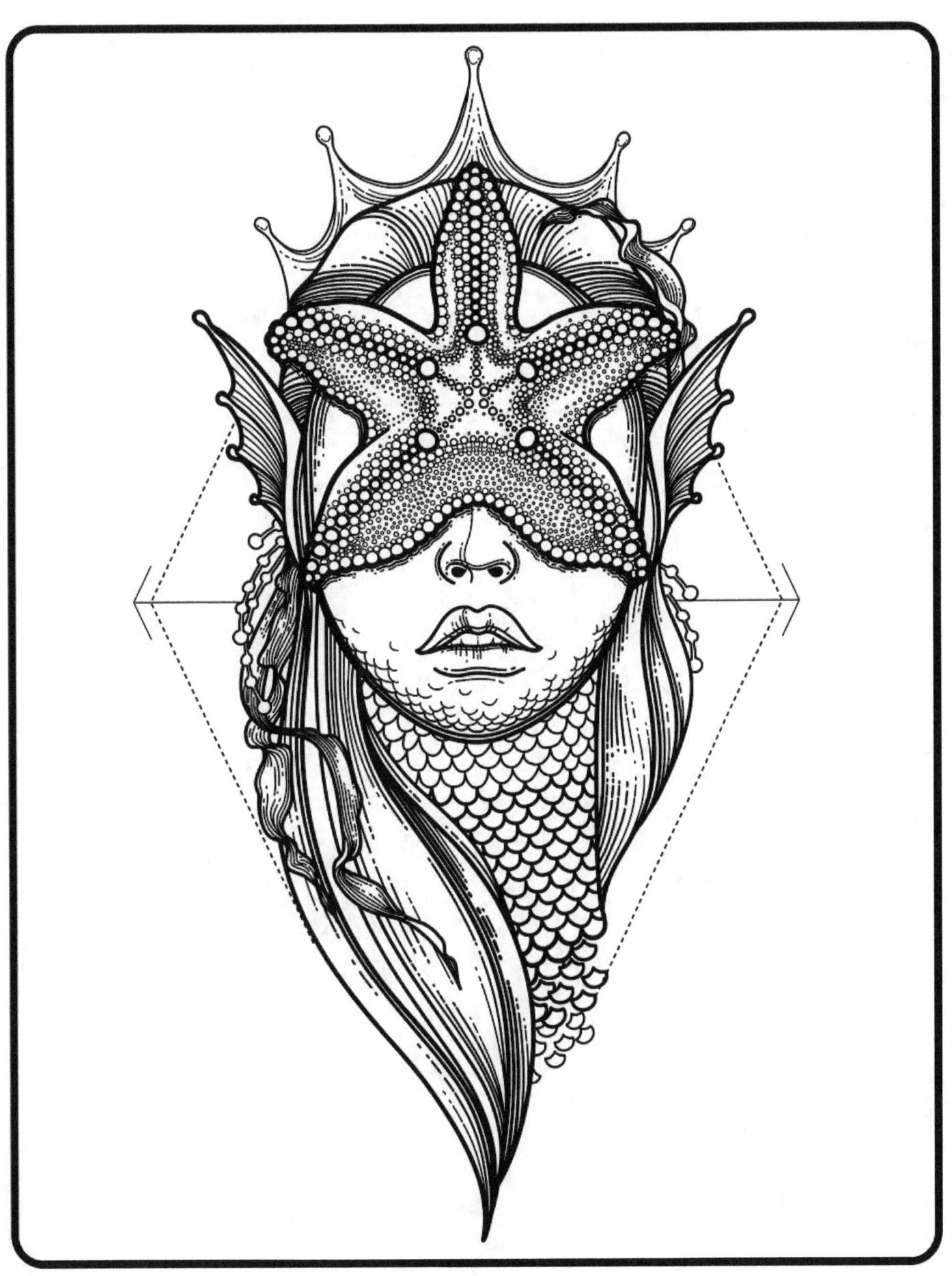

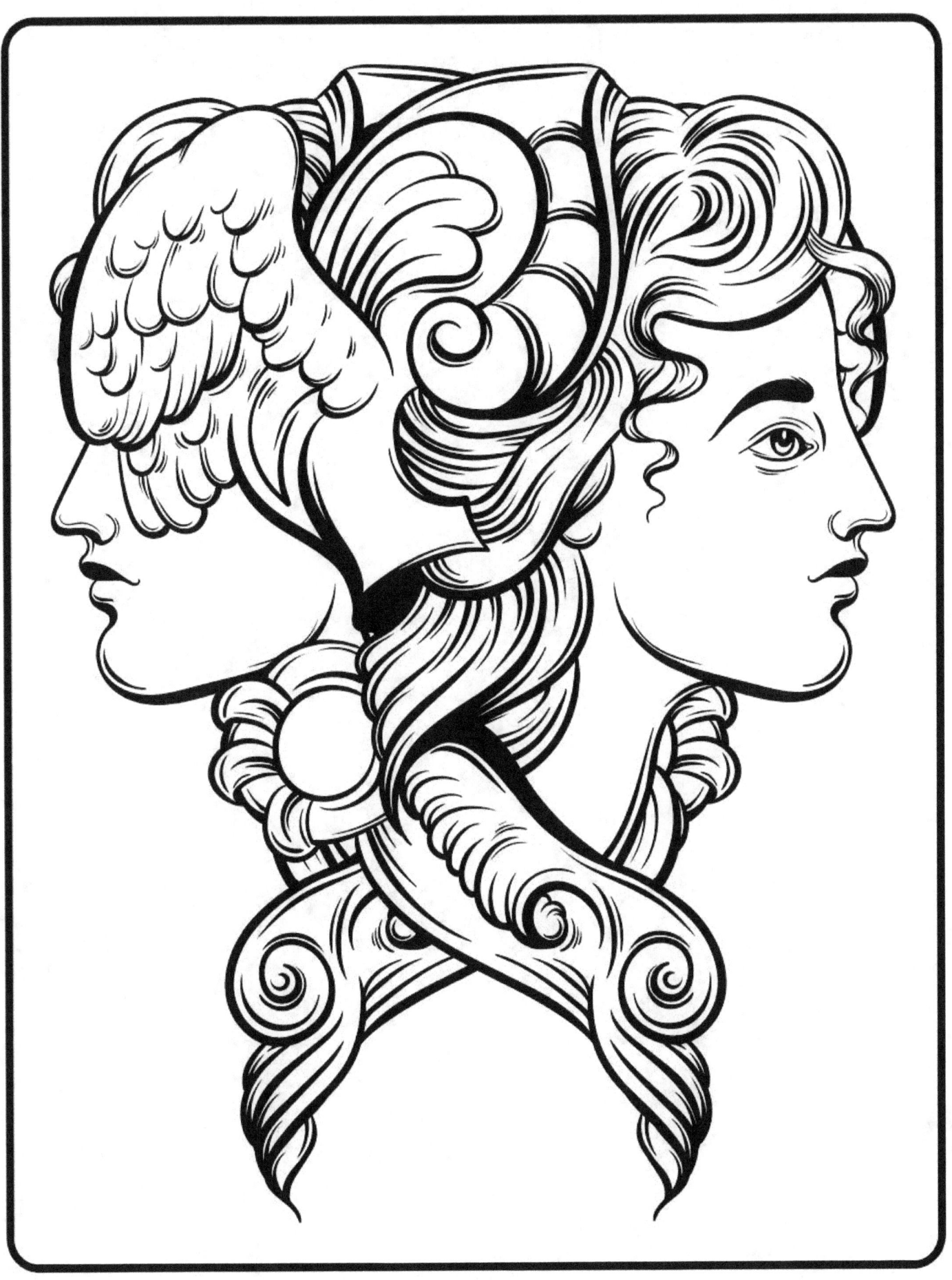

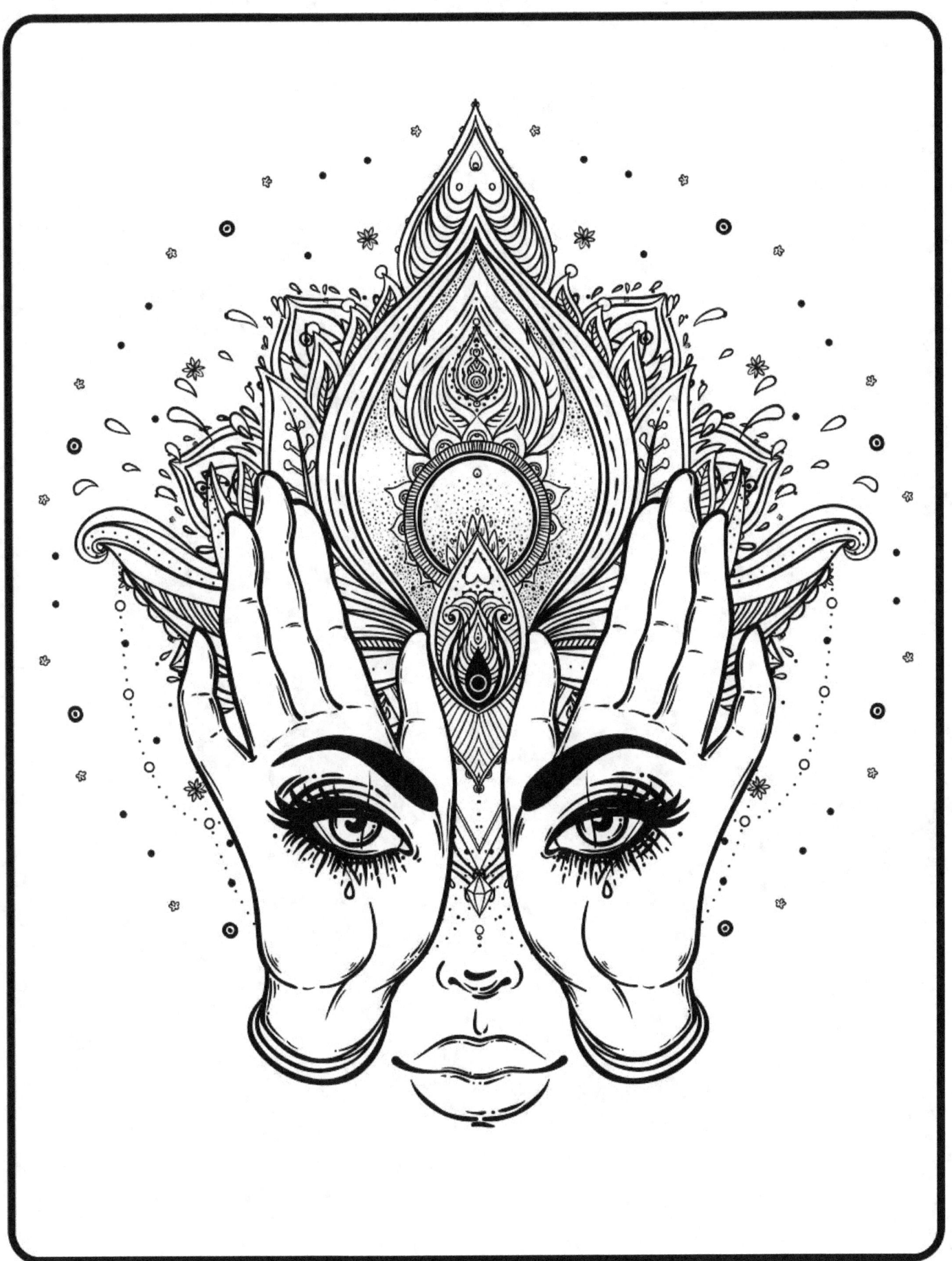

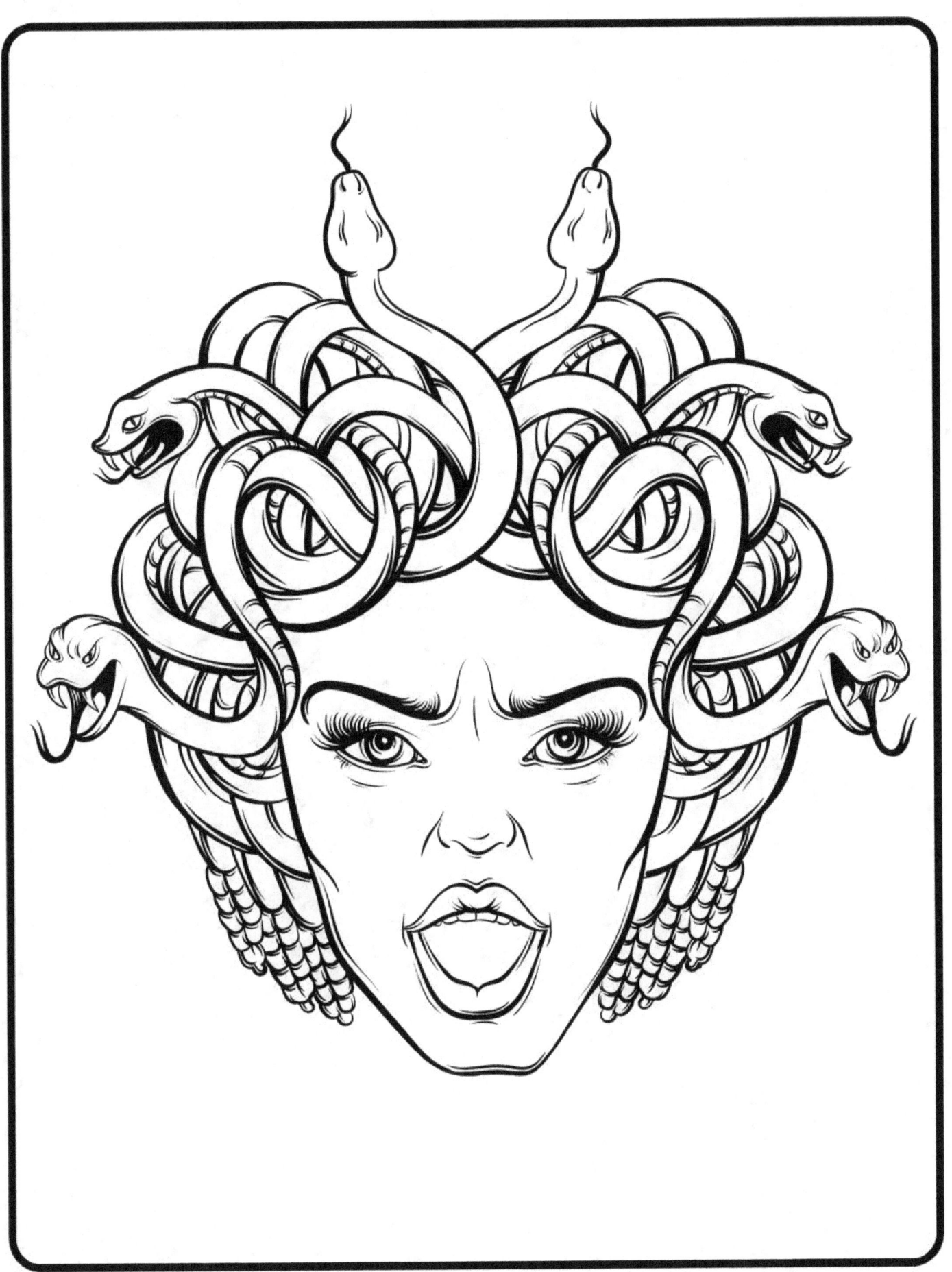

MORE COLORING BOOKS FROM KATRIN STARK

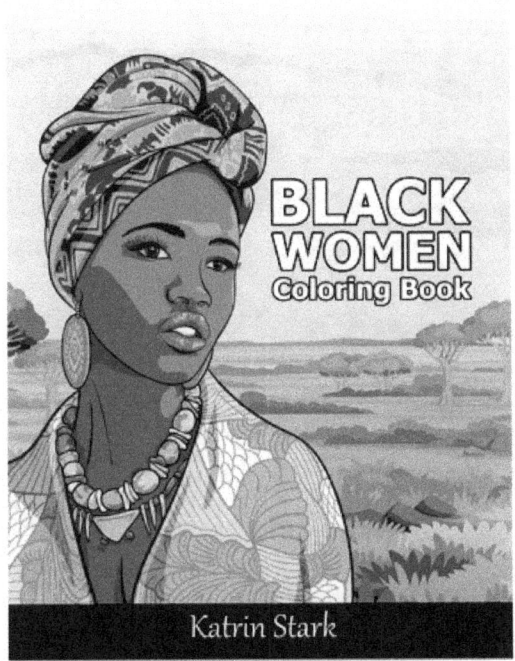
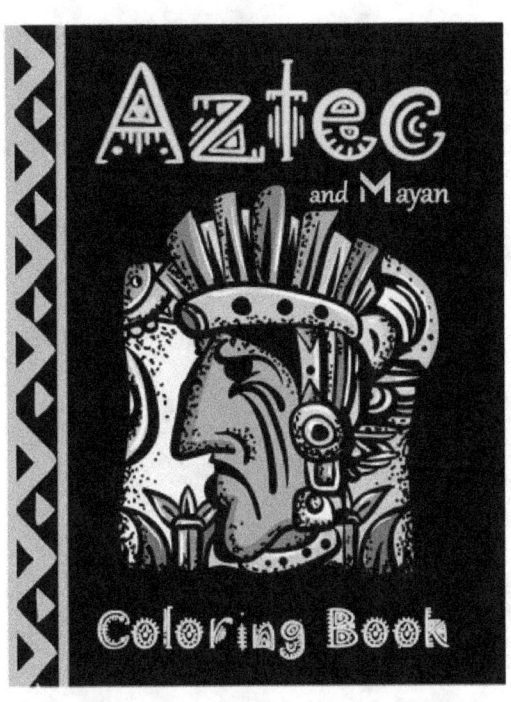
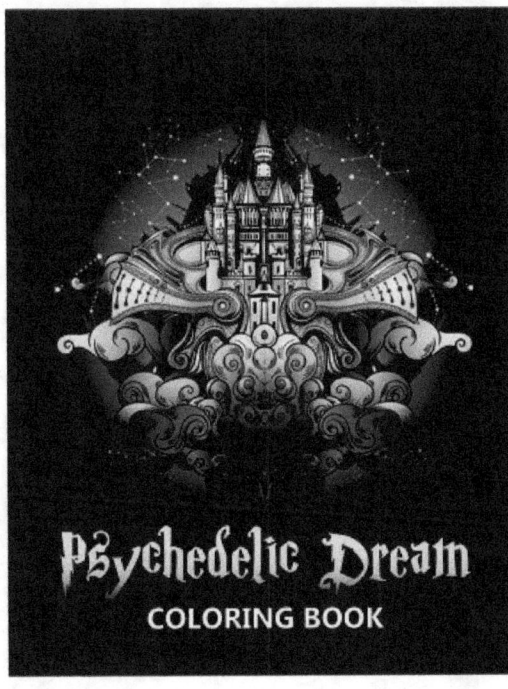
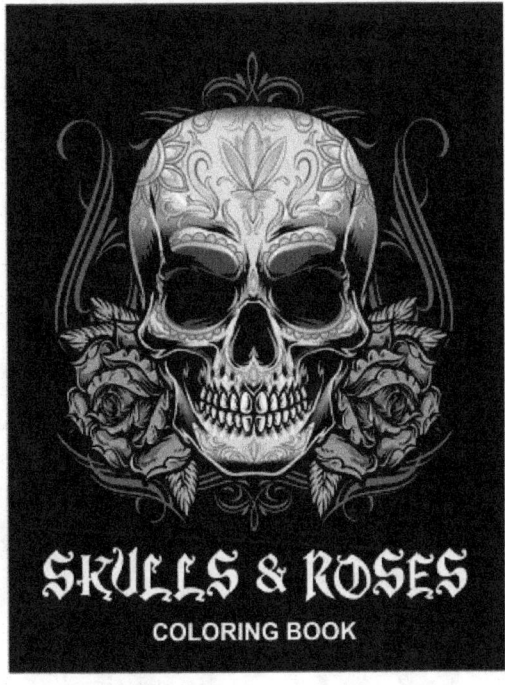

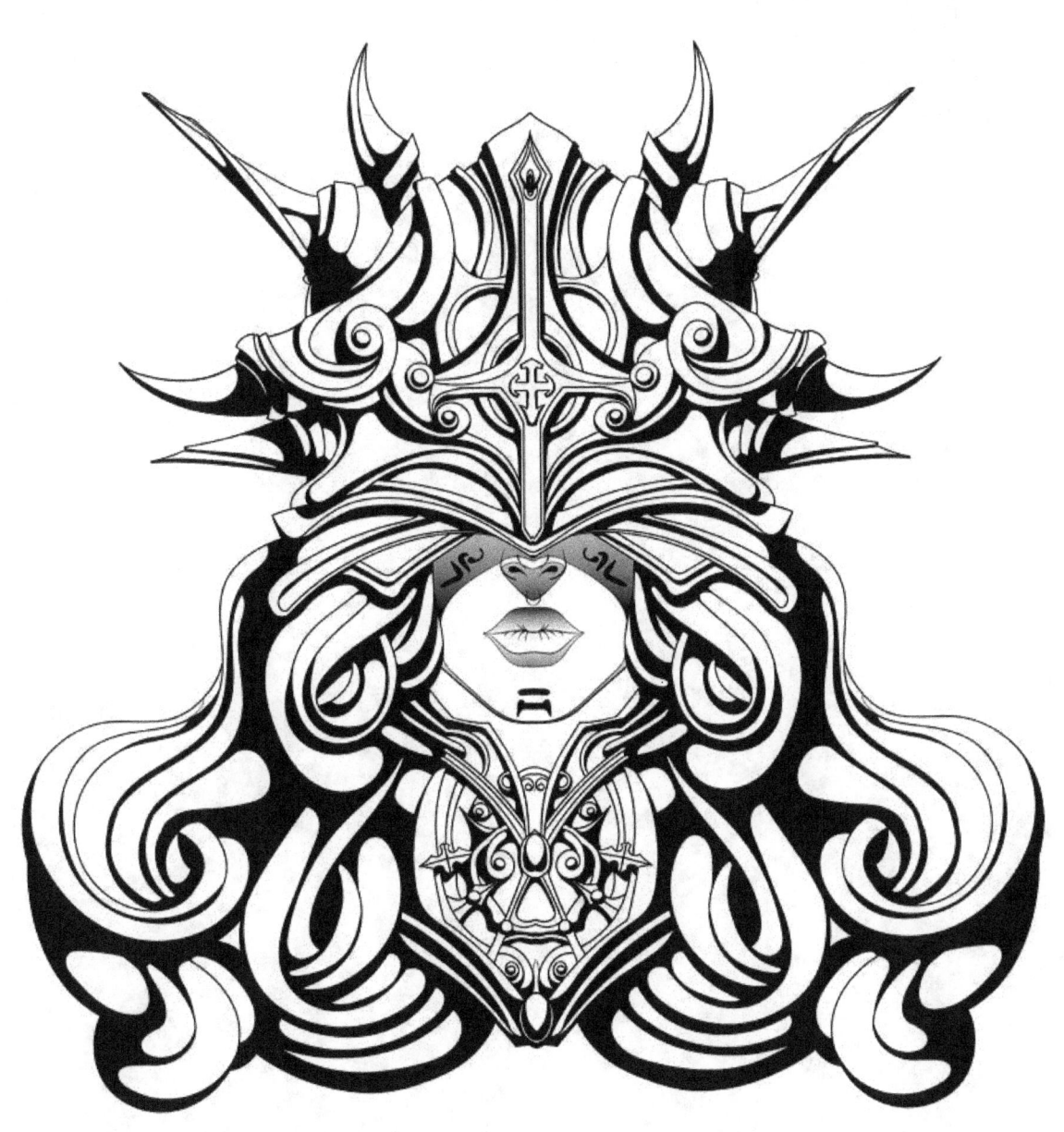

Thank you for buying this book

If you like the book, please consider leaving a review,
it will help author to create better books in the future

www.amazon.com/Katrin-Stark
www.amazon.co.uk/Katrin-Stark

www.ingramcontent.com/pod-product-compliance
Lightning Source LLC
Chambersburg PA
CBHW080524220526
45465CB00006B/2588